*Praise for 'l*

"In reading Jack's book I felt lik~ _ _ _ _ _ _ _ _ _ _
camp. A hard-nosed and effective approach to spiritual growth
that is not a luxury, but rather a necessity, in these troubled
times. I would be honored to go into spiritual combat with Jack
any day.
 If you want to take your spiritual values into the real world,
follow THIS leader and the advice he shares with the intensity
of a drill sergeant and the compassion of a spiritual icon."
**Dick Grace, Former US Marine,**
**Buddhist Activist and**
**Founder Grace Family Vineyards**

"Jack Schropp was sure paying attention while he was taking
in the life lessons of BEING a SEAL.
 Now the rest of the world can be lucky enough to learn
from Jack's insights and experience."
**Governor Jesse Ventura**

"A beautiful oxymoron . . . SEAL for Peace? A fascinating
book for men and women that celebrates World Peace, and
stresses the importance of taking action in one's life
—RIGHT NOW!"
**Donald Ziraldo**
**President of Inniskillin Wines and**
**Recipient of 'The Order of Canada'**

Unbeatable speaks the truth. Even if you're not ready to make
the commitment, read the book once to get the basic concept.
Then, when you hit rock bottom, start on page one.
**Laura Post, age 18**

"I particularly liked Jack's description of an "operator." I met many guys in recon who fit that description and could get ANYTHING done that needed to be done."
**J. Barrie Graham, President and CEO,**
**Exchange Bank**

"Unbeatable is destined to be a classic. Never before have I been given the opportunity to learn first-hand the 'secrets' behind the extraordinary success of the Navy SEALs, and get the blueprint on how to apply them to my own life. Recreating my life as extraordinary began with opening this book."
**Tari Stork, Public Relations**

I had the opportunity to read this book and do the exercises with my husband, and at a time when we were challenged in our relationship. The book and exercises opened up conversations about our marriage that we never would have had otherwise. Life-long therapy can't give people what they can get in Jack's book and in less than 200 pages. It's the best investment for any couple looking to have an extraordinary relationship.
**Dina Robb, Pharmaceutical Medical Representative.**

For more information on Jack Schropp, purchasing UNBEATABLE, his programs, and keynote speaking engagements, go to:

www.jackschropp.com

# UNBEATABLE

Stay 'Unbeatable'!

# UNBEATABLE

*Recreate Your Life*
*As Extraordinary Using*
*the Secrets of a Navy Seal*

## Jack Schropp
Commander of the Navy SEALs (Ret.)

To order additional copies of this book, go to:
www.jackschropp.com
UNBEATABLE is available through your local bookstore.
(Distributed by Ingram Distribution)
20155

# CONTENTS

*Human brotherhood is not just a goal.*
*It is a condition on which our way of life depends.*
*The question for our time is not whether all men are brothers.*
*That question has been answered by God who placed us on this earth together.*
*The question is whether we have the strength and the will to make the brotherhood of man the guiding principle of our daily lives.*

John F. Kennedy

*I hope that people will finally come to realize that there is only one 'race'—the human race— and that we are all members of it.*

Margaret Atwood

*War is at best barbarism . . . its glory is all moonshine.*
*It is only those that have neither fired a shot nor heard the shrieks and groans of the wounded who cry aloud for blood, more vengeance, more desolation.*
*War is hell.*

William Tecumseh Sherman (June 19, 1879)
(Spoken 15 years after the end of the American Civil War.)

*The grim fact, however, is that we prepare for war like precocious giants and for peace like retarded pygmies.*

Lester B. Pearson

*Any person who is offended by anything anyone says requires immediate sentencing to fifteen to twenty years in a four-man cell with George Carlin, Richard Pryor and Dennis Miller!*

# Preface

## How This Book Came About

I have always been at home in the water. Maybe it's a womb thing . . . The Navy claims (by their diploma) that they trained me to be a frogman (Navy SEAL.) The reality? I was a frogman waiting to happen.

At age sixteen I looked at my life and figured I was pretty good at a few things. I could swim well, particularly underwater. In those days, during the summer, I spent all my free time at Lake Conewago across the road from my home in the small village of Mt. Gretna, Pennsylvania. I thought, *"If I could somehow get a job swimming all the time, it would be the perfect life!"* The only options I knew were being a lifeguard or a Navy frogman. My parents encouraged me to do something they felt worthwhile, such as working at the family newspaper. I considered working with my father or even being an actor. Then I read, For Whom the Bell Tolls, by Ernest Hemingway, and my destiny was set. In Hemingway's book, the protagonist, Robert Jordan, was a demolition expert who stood for a noble cause against the tyranny of Nazi Germany and Fascist Italy during the Spanish Civil War. I could use my ability as a swimmer to learn how to be a member of the Underwater Demolition Teams (UDT). All for a noble cause . . . defending my country . . . I could get paid to swim and blow things up! When I learned that frogman training was difficult, I felt more challenged, just as I had felt when, at ages eleven to twelve, I used to defend our lake from the rowdy teenagers who came from the surrounding cities of Lancaster, Reading and Harrisburg. These teens would harass and bully the younger kids. So, I launched sneak attacks and ambushes, swimming underwater out to the rafts, then suddenly rising up, grabbing a teen from behind and pulling him underwater! I'd let the teen struggle for a bit, then release him and swim away. The subsequent sound of splashing told me the other teens had jumped into the water to catch me. Along the lake bottom I swam, toward and under a distant pier. (I also used to spread rumors that snapping turtles lived under the piers. I knew the teens would never think that this was where I was hiding. Later in life I realized I was using psychological warfare.) The rowdy teens NEVER caught me. It was my self-appointed duty, as one of the heavier kids in my age group, to defend my buddies at the lake. Most certainly I was a SEAL waiting to happen.

While, at the young age of sixteen years old, I was deciding my destiny to be a Navy frogman, little did I know of the adventures, mishaps, trials and tribulations I had in store. Gladly forfeiting many teenage benefits, such as joining a fraternity or attending a co-ed college, I certainly reaped other benefits that I could have never foreseen. On many occasions and under extreme conditions, I had the privilege of seeing people at their finest. Certain aspects of my personality (some folks claim I lack one) were enhanced; others atrophied.

From all this, as well as from my education in other than strictly military matters, such as having three ex-wives, five children, three grandchildren, extensive travel experience, attending seminars, training to lead seminars, and being in relationship with hundreds of thousands of people, I realized something . . .

---

 *It takes little effort and absolutely no intelligence to see the differences between human beings. We are all different. Even one's dog or cat distinguishes between people and/or other animals.*

---

Our world is organized around people's differences, all of which are accidents of birth (culture, language, religion, race, economic status, etc.) It is these differences that are at the root of wars. In 1975, I first became interested in, and then committed to, finding the similarities that exist among all people. Americans, Russians, Koreans, Vietnamese, Arabs or Afghanis have many commonalities. People simply have different sets of cultural values and different perspectives about life. I had spent a good part of my adult life defending and being right about MY cultural values and MY perspective about life. Who said I was right? Or as my mother had frequently said to me when I was a kid, *"Who made you the judge and jury?"* I never had a retort for that one. (The answer is NO ONE.)

I had been living like a train, racing along narrow rails through my life and headed in one, limited direction. AND I was unaware of this. Then I had the privilege of participating in an intensive transformational workshop over a couple of weekends. In this workshop, I began to look at my life, and from one perspective, account for why I was who I was and why I had chosen to do what I did. This insight had me question the direction of my life. I asked myself, *"Am I ever going to kill or capture enough communists to make a difference for my country, and for that matter, the world?"* (Little did I know how irrelevant this commitment would become with respect to our new relationship with communists today.) I stepped off the train. This epiphany was the source of my retirement from the Navy in 1982. I retired with the rank of commander, having graduated from the United States Naval Academy, completed three tours of duty in Vietnam, two tours as a commanding officer of Underwater Demolition Teams (now called SEAL Teams) and overall, a highly successful career as a Naval Special Warfare officer.

I boarded another train, this one headed in the direction of honoring and supporting ALL people and to making a difference, in a peaceful manner, not only for U.S. citizens, but for ALL people around the world. I had realized that I no longer had to subscribe to the insanity of preparing for and fighting wars as a way to reach peace! This now occurred to me as insane as burning down a forest so as to eliminate arson or as one winning the heavyweight boxing championship of the world while suffering major brain damage. Where is the win? Through many conversations with people from various social, economic and cultural backgrounds, and over time, I brought closure and completion to my past and my duties as a warrior. Over time I gained peace of mind and recreated my life.

For the next twenty years, I trained and then worked as a human development trainer for the largest off-campus educational company in the world, leading seminars for the public, corporations, organizations, and special interest groups. I estimate that I led seminars for more than one hundred thousand people worldwide during this time.

In July 2001, I led my last seminar, and then spent ten days with two of my five children (Erin and Christopher) and my partner, Shari, on an island in Georgian Bay, Canada. While there, I started to get excited about retiring and spending the remainder of my years at home with my family. (I had spent most of my two careers traveling the world.)

Arriving home I realized, to a much greater degree, that my children and Shari had lives of their own. While my children liked that their dad was home if needed, preferably in the background, they spent most of their time with friends, just as I had done when I was a teenager. My daily routine consisted of two-hour workouts at the gym, sitting on my front porch in shorts and a T-shirt, premium cigar in hand, and the first of many great books on my lap. Retirement felt awesome! No hotels. No airplanes. Life was quiet. Life was good!

. . . until September 11th, 2001

Retirement lasted less than a month! On the morning of September 11, 2001, I turned on the TV to watch the morning news. The first plane had already crashed into the World Trade Center and re-runs of the 'accident' were being highlighted. When the second plane crashed into the second World Trade tower, I realized these were not accidents, but an attack. Obviously by terrorists.

With the collapse of the towers, followed by people's pandemonium, shock and grief over the next couple of days, I experienced helplessness, sadness and rage. I also thought about all the energy, money and time that the government agencies had put toward anti-terrorist activities and agendas in the previous twenty years that had now proven to be a failure—unless you were in the counter-terrorist business and counted your small battles won prior to September 11, 2001.

I felt compelled to contribute in some way. In our American culture, retirees are rarely, if ever, given the opportunity to resume active duty. In attempting to do something worthwhile, I contacted the U.S. Marshals' Service, believing I could volunteer my service as a marshal aboard airplanes. Unfortunately, I was too old by twenty-one years, thus eliminating that possibility. (I still think it is a great idea for retired SEALs, Army Special Forces and Marines to provide this service on a volunteer, unpaid basis. Among other things, these former warriors could disrupt enemy profiling by being outside the stereotypical 'air marshal' look. On top of this, one's age does not hamper nor negate the countless years of training, experience and ability in disarming terrorists. This idea could also allow for greater manpower, higher security and reduced costs for the Air Marshal Program.)

Over the next few weeks, I watched the news morning, noon and night. In the aftermath of the attacks, and from my perspective, North Americans were devastated, their lives forever changed. With fluctuating financial markets, a decline in the economy, loss of businesses and loss of jobs, North Americans felt fearful and defeated. Was this where I could possibly make a difference? Through my training and experience as a commander of the Navy SEALs, and as a trainer in human development, I had learned that:

*Everyone has what it takes to be unbeatable in the face of impossible odds.*

Most people have never been tested on a SUSTAINED BASIS, yet many have acted in an extraordinary manner when confronted with a crisis, such as a natural disaster or family emergency. These circumstances are hopefully few and usually occur as a result of outside forces pressing in on our lives. People who operate as extraordinary on a regular basis, and who have been tested, understand how capable they are and perform as unbeatable.

While North Americans struggled to survive after the horror of September 11, 2001, they were hit once again with adversity—this time in March, 2003. The devastating news of the U.S. War on Iraq was too much for most people to accept. Barely recovering from this shocking news, we were then struck by the onset of the Severe Acute Respiratory Syndrome (SARS) epidemic, most seriously in Canada.

How can North Americans cope, let alone thrive, in the face of this multi-faceted onslaught: the continuing war on global terrorism, the aftermath of September 11, the War on Iraq, SARS, and the corporate meltdown in current times brought on by personal greed and/or lack of integrity? Moreover, how can North Americans thrive in the face of ANY adversity life throws their way, without having access to the appropriate training to do so—the training to be unbeatable?

I wrote this book to provide you, the reader, with a vantage point from which to look at your life, for what could make a difference for you in your life. I am committed to providing you with the attributes (secrets) needed for you to possess an unbeatable attitude in the face of ALL adversity life throws your way.

The research for this book included working with human development experts and Navy SEALs, re-reading the many books written by and about Navy SEALs (many with whom I have served) and watching recent Navy SEAL documentary videos. I also looked into my own past, at my experiences and memories of former shipmates, to determine the attributes that exist at the core of a Navy SEAL's being. Over time I assembled a long list of attributes and analyzed them closely. What began as a long list was reduced to twelve secrets of a Navy SEAL . . . not DOING the job of a Navy SEAL, as this requires one to be of a specific age and undergo the Basic Underwater, Demolition and SEAL Training (BUD/S) in Coronado, California. Rather, this book imparts the 'moment by moment' essence of BEING a SEAL, so that you may also be unbeatable and extraordinary in whatever you do in your life. I would venture to say that the attitude and attributes of a Navy SEAL are similar to those possessed by many NATO Special Forces Units, such as the Joint Task Force Two (JTF-2), a highly secretive team of operators in the Canadian Armed Forces believed to be used for counter terrorism and hostage rescue missions and activities. By the same token, my goal is that you use these attributes to being unbeatable in a peaceful way to enhance your own life and contribute to others.

Having also undergone the intense emotional and intellectual training through my participation and employment with my former company, having been coached extensively, and having coached and worked with thousands of people, I am able to convey these attributes (secrets) from my own, distinct point of view. This book is about the attitude and attributes of BEING a Navy SEAL, developed throughout BUD/S Training and polished during service in several of the operational SEAL teams (working SEALs). My sole intention is that you benefit from this information by considering how this attitude and these attributes (secrets) might positively impact your life.

PART ONE

# BUD/S Training . . .
# To recreate your life
# as extraordinary using
# the secrets of a Navy
# SEAL!

# INTRODUCTION

# How does one become a Navy SEAL?

# Introduction

## How does one become a Navy SEAL?

*When you send a clerk on business to a distant province, a man of rigid morals is not your best choice.*

—Ihara Saikaku (1642-1693)

Most people are intrigued by what SEALs do, like dangerous and covert missions. What few know is that SEALs must BE a certain way to do extraordinary missions to succeed. At any time, in any environment, under adverse conditions, SEALs succeed more often than not because they possess an attitude and a set of attributes called to BE UNBEATABLE!

To give you access to being unbeatable in your own life, you will need to have a foundation of understanding of the Navy SEAL training program called BUD/S. It is through BUD/S that an ordinary person develops himself into being an extraordinary one—a Navy SEAL.

BUD/S Training is considered the most arduous in the Armed Forces. To successfully complete the training, a trainee repeatedly demonstrates BEING unbeatable in the face of his own repeated failings and by the instructors' unrelenting pressure. The SEAL instructors take committed and highly qualified (physically, medically and academically) trainees and run them through demanding physical, emotional and mental exercises designed to press them beyond human tolerance. No matter what reason a trainee has for wanting to be a Navy SEAL, it is completely insufficient to survive this training process.

A SEAL is always choosing to accomplish his mission with the quality of a committed, trained volunteer who knows he is at risk, often with no backup or support. Sometimes he represents only himself or his team with his existence denied by his country.

Those who succeed over their excuses experience an indescribable sense of accomplishment. Successful graduates demonstrate to themselves, their classmates, and instructors, over a six-month training program, day after day, night after night, that they are bigger than their self-limiting beliefs. The instructors attempt to cause the candidate to 'ring the bell,' a public event that denotes quitting. Trainees are rarely thrown out; they are pressed until they quit. It is one thing to do pushups when rested. It is quite another to do them when you are at the point of exhaustion. Consequently, a typical class will have an attrition (failure) rate of between 66 and 90 percent!

Upon emerging from BUD/S, the SEAL knows his limits and knows he can accomplish future missions with his fellow trainees. He also sees his instructors in a new light, not as tormentors, but rather as coaches or mentors committed to producing Navy SEALs. The successful trainees have demonstrated standing fast to their commitment, no matter what the world throws at them or what they throw at themselves. Commitment is not about wanting something badly. Commitment is not only about saying, *"I am committed."* Commitment is also not trying REALLY hard, doing your best, or merely saying, *"I'll do it."* Commitment, in this paradigm, is simply doing what you said you would do and remaining in the training beyond reason.

---

 *Commitment is choosing in each moment.*

---

This kind of commitment keeps the prospective SEAL from quitting. BUD/S consists of the individual trainee operating by keeping his word at its most basic level—one moment, one day, and one evolution (exercise) at a time. To remain in BUD/S beyond reason, to remain when the sensible route seems to be to quit, many of the successful trainees have had as their personal expression of commitment, *"The only way they will get me out of here is to kill me!"* In other words, their commitment was worth their lives. They then proceeded to live this statement, moment by moment, hour by hour, day by day, for six months.

Upon graduating from BUD/S, the new SEAL enters the Teams, the organizations of existing SEALs. He begins all over again, demonstrating for another six months that he has what it takes, and that he will display it reliably, at any time, under all circumstances, anywhere in the world. The new SEAL knows that while he has done the impossible for an unreasonably long period in BUD/S, he cannot thrive alone when operating under adverse conditions. The new SEAL becomes a member of an operational SEAL team, a group of men who can each stand on their own, is dependable without question, and can contribute these qualities to the team's success.

Each SEAL, regardless of rank, participates in the

design and preparation of missions. The officers and enlisted men train together, thus sharing an extraordinary level of communication and relatedness. Having trained so thoroughly and repeatedly, SEALs know that missions rarely go exactly as planned. JUST like life! So SEALs consider the big picture, from their reliance on and cooperation with the sailors who man the boats/planes/ships that deliver or extract them, to the civilian authority for which they ultimately work. Many paradoxes exist in a SEAL's world, not the least of which is being independent and dependent at the same time.

All SEAL training is done with the deck stacked against them. So, by design, combat is less demanding than the training, leaving no alternative but to excel in the execution of their missions. Most people would think that combat is more difficult than the training. This is the same principle in professional football, at least for championship teams. That is, their preparation and training is far more extensive than the game itself. No matter what the situation, under the worst circumstances, SEALs know they can survive and excel by being steadfast, tough and improvisational, and delivering results with overwhelming and lightning-fast impact, and then getting out unscathed to move onto the next mission. When in trouble or separated from his team, the SEAL knows that as long as he is alive, there is always a way to carry out his mission.

---

    *There is always a way to succeed!*

---

From these physical training programs, SEALs emerge with an extraordinary attitude and an understanding of their own attributes—the secrets!

Are YOU ready to undergo your own BUD/S program to recreate your life as extraordinary? If so, you will want to consider committing to the idea that . . . no matter what the universe throws at you, or what you throw at yourself, despite any future situation and under the worst circumstances, you WILL use these secrets to find a way to thrive in the face of repeated failings and adversity.

Are you ready to volunteer for BUD/S? Are you ready to fulfill your own life's mission with overwhelming and lightning-fast impact? If so, let us get started . . .

**You're ready for BUD/S indoctrination!**

# CHAPTER ONE

# Indoctrination
# (Why the secrets?)

# Chapter One

## Indoctrination

## (Why the secrets?)

*The important and decisive factor in life is not what happens to us, but the attitude we take toward what happens. The surest revelation of one's character is the way one bears one's suffering. Circumstances and situations may color life, but by the grace of God, we have been given the power to choose what that color shall be.*
*The effect that misfortune, handicap, sickness, and sorrow have upon life is determined by the way in which we meet them.*

—Charles R. Woodson

For BUD/S indoctrination, you'll want to understand how the process to being unbeatable works. The process in being unbeatable is not about you needing to change yourself to be different at some point in the future. You are perfect just the way that you are right now. You have access, right now, to take action, right now, to be unbeatable in your life. After all, the only time you are ever participating in your life is . . . right now!

If you're interested in being unbeatable, you might want to start by asking yourself a question: "Who am I, right now, in this moment, with respect to the matter of my own success?" (I'm referring to success in your romantic relationship, in your career and/or within your family.)

I'll ask the question again . . .

Who are you in the matter of your own success?

See if you can, in your mind, come up with one word or phrase to describe who you are in the matter of your own success right now. For example, some of the possible places in which you could be are:

---

- Uncertain.
- Doing the best you can.
- You wish you had better or more success in your business.
- You could be hopeful.
- You could be satisfied.
- Disheartened.
- Depressed.
- Ready to pack it in.
- Frustrated.
- Biding your time.
- Sick of failing.
- Sick and tired.
- Ready to quit.
- Looking for a new relationship or business technique.

---

As you read through this book, keep this word or

phrase in your mind. While you will have access to the attributes of a Navy SEAL, the idea is for you to implement them in a way that adds positive and peaceful action to your own life and to contribute to those you love.

## THE CHAPTERS

As you move through the information on the secrets in each chapter, I suggest you keep a highlighter pen handy, to mark the sentences that ring true for you. Later on, go back and look at these sentences again, and look at your life THROUGH these ideas. Apply the material to your own life instead of merely understanding it. This will allow you to see, first hand, where you may have failed in the past, and where you might want to implement the secrets into your present life—this time to achieve success in any given area of your life that is presently not working.

## THE SECRETS:

The secrets to being unbeatable have remained concealed from general knowledge until now. Just as there is a difference between the description or explanation of swimming and one actually 'being' a swimmer, the U.S. Navy employs a rigorous physical, mental and psychological training program designed to produce men who will BE Navy SEALs. In other words, trainees get the secrets experientially. In this book you will have access to these secrets through your own BUD/S program.

We all know that men dominate the military world— specifically the Navy SEALs. (Many would say men born with too much testosterone!) This certainly might be true. But contrary to popular belief, the trainees who make it through BUD/S are not necessarily the most testosterone driven, biggest or strongest of the volunteers. In fact, the trainees who seemingly have it the easiest in the beginning are often the first to quit the training. Those who make it through possess and polish certain attributes (secrets) for life. These attributes exist in ALL people, men and women alike. The secrets are universal. Oprah Winfrey, for example, has shown the world that she is unbeatable. To be unbeatable does not mean Oprah is free from failing. The opposite is true. Oprah is unbeatable because she fails repeatedly and yet continues to fulfill her commitments and achieve her desired goals. What makes Oprah extraordinary is that she continues to recreate her life despite repeated failings—while the world watches through a magnifying glass and scrutinizes her every move. This is truly extraordinary!

The SEAL secrets are the attitude and attributes of a Navy SEAL, not a priest, minister, guru, monk, motivational speaker, policeman, lawyer or doctor. The secrets are also not to replace any religious or cultural philosophies, beliefs, principles or ideals you already possess. Each trainee who becomes a Navy SEAL has his own philosophies and religious beliefs, including those who are agnostic or atheist. The SEAL secrets discussed may coincide with some of your personal beliefs, philosophies, principles or ideals, but you, the reader, not me, decide upon this.

While enumerated sequentially into chapters (one after the other), the secrets in reality, will overlap and work together and are dependent upon one another. For example, to be proficient at the secret of being 'resourceful' without first mastering the secret of being an 'operator,' could and has proved, at times, troublesome for the individual SEAL and his teammates. When they begin BUD/S, the trainees are at their own level of proficiency and effectiveness with the secrets, and they develop them at a pace sufficient to meet the BUD/S standards. If their pace is insufficient, they are no longer trainees. Once in an operational SEAL team, the SEAL continues to develop, hone and practice these attributes.

Some of these secrets may be underdeveloped within you. Or, you may understand them conceptually, believing that you have already mastered them. Take note—the secrets you think you have mastered might be the ones in which you are the weakest. The secrets you think need polishing might be the ones that have been dormant within you.

Here is a simple test: look at your relationship between your current commitments and your results. If these are misaligned, *"You've got some thinkin' to do, Lucy!" (Desi Arnaz)*

We almost always see other people's weaknesses more readily than our own. Be true to yourself, even consult with your best friend, and determine which secrets are missing and which ones you underutilize. The idea is to continually develop them all and have them work harmoniously in your life so that you can be unbeatable as adversity strikes. By the way, no one can force you to develop these secrets. Only YOU can develop them if you so choose. The final exam for this book is the rest of your life.

Do you have what it takes to be unbeatable, to be extraordinary in your life? You do. No matter who you are, you ALREADY possess all of these attributes. Whether or not you want to polish them or employ them is up to you. In case your mother forgot to tell you, it is all right to live as you are. We all end up toasted or planted or cryogenically frozen anyway, with our friends and relatives talking about us at a restaurant brunch following the funeral service . . . at least for five minutes . . . and then they move on to more interesting topics.

---

*As long as you are alive, you are always playing the game of life. It is up to you on how you choose to play it.*

---

There are NO answers to life's mysteries. In other words, this is not the process for you if you're looking to me to provide you with answers to your problems, or to give you a step-by-step, detailed guide on how to function. Advice, ultimately, NEVER works anyway. As human beings we must all learn from our own REPEATED failings. YOU are undertaking the BUD/S program, and it is up to YOU to do the evolutions (exercises)—that is if you are interested in implementing new structures into the areas of your life that presently DO NOT work.

On more than one occasion, I've heard people say that a specific workshop, seminar or book did not make a difference for them. People often feel inspired or motivated by the writer or speaker's enthusiasm during a seminar or workshop. But after a week or so, they quickly fall back into old habits. As a result, they determine that the book, workshop, seminar or speaker had proven ineffective. This is a justification so that they can avoid being responsible for their own lives and/or capabilities. The fact is this: workshops, seminars and books are vehicles. Ultimately, YOU are fully responsible for implementing any new insights into your life on a sustained basis. No one can hold your hand to make your life workable, least of all extraordinary. The only obstacle that might get in your way is your OWN cynicism or resignation.

Where do your feelings fall into the realm of being unbeatable? Feelings are an integral part of who we are, and although I will touch on the subject of them from a SEAL's perspective, this book is not homage to them. I'll leave the world of understanding one's feelings to Dr. Phil. He's a master in this area. The SEAL secrets I'm sharing are to have you be unbeatable in any endeavor you pursue—whether you **FEEL** like it or not!

## THE SUBTITLE: RECREATE YOUR LIFE AS EXTRAORDINARY

The book's subtitle is *Recreate Your Life as Extraordinary Using the Secrets of a Navy SEAL*. What does it mean to recreate one's life as extraordinary? To create is to bring something into existence from nothing. When young, we begin to create, mostly unwittingly, who we are, with all of our hopes and dreams, then promptly forget we did this. In failing over and over again, we become discouraged and resigned into living a reasonable, manageable, comfortable and ordinary life.

*Success covers a multitude of sins.*
—George Bernard Shaw

To RE-create one's life as extraordinary is to be uncomfortable and begin this process anew—this time playing life's game at the level of an adult. Why do I say adult? Because it is only possible to recreate one's life by first distinguishing those childish— UNWORKABLE—behaviors, attitudes and expressions that have been unwittingly running one's life. This does not mean giving up being youthful or enjoying the 'kid' in you. That's workable! To be extraordinary is to give up the behaviors that do not work for you. You will, if interested, continue to do this throughout your life, moment by moment. The process for being unbeatable does not focus on the information or details concerning our 'inner child' . . . I'll leave that to psychologists and psychiatrists. Suffice it to say that when you have the courage to look at the way you are behaving in life, you will notice that you have been behaving these same unworkable ways since childhood. When life just doesn't work, you might start to see that some of your childish behaviors and expectations are, at their very foundation, the cause of your disruptions. For a light brush stroke of this, simply listen to all the things that you say to yourself and to others that include the phrases:

- I WANT
- I DON'T WANT
- YOU CAN'T MAKE ME
- ALWAYS
- NEVER
- EVERYBODY
- ALL THE TIME
- SHOULD or SHOULDN'T . . .

Are these not the phrases you hear kids declaring? Whenever you hear yourself using these words and/or phrases, you are in the meadow of a million bulls!

To recreate one's life as extraordinary is to acknowledge failing as healthy. Failing is an integral element in the art of being unbeatable. It is also a secret. The more comfortable you become at failing, the less time you'll need to recover. The faster you recover from each failure, the faster you'll be able to RE-create your life to be extraordinary. If you are uncomfortable with this idea, no doubt you are someone who is interested in winning all the time. If winning is all that interests you, I suggest you find a game of which you are currently proficient and keep playing it. This will ensure that you will constantly win. Is this extraordinary? No. The game of winning ALL the time will eventually leave you dissatisfied and make no difference for you or anyone else. You will attain a momentary flush of success upon winning. I call this glee. The problem is, to experience glee, the stakes must progressively get bigger, better or higher. Glee is insatiable and requires that someone win and someone lose.

To be extraordinary is to accept and embrace repeated failings, recover as quickly as possible—that is let go of all your reasons and excuses to justify the failing—then move on to carry out your commitment or to move onto your next goal and ultimately to move on with your life. What does it mean to be extraordinary? It means living a life that is not ordinary and going beyond what is usual, expected, comfortable or normal. Being extraordinary, as a matter of routine, will offer you the possibility of having all of your dreams come true.

Keep in mind that the greatest hurdle to being extraordinary is to believe you already are! What might your life be like if you try out these secrets? You will have the opportunity to acquire the following:

---

- Access to recovering immediately from failing.
- Increased effectiveness, i.e., more things go the way YOU SAY, instead of the the way it seems they are inevitably going.

---

- Inventiveness in areas where you haven't been inventive.
- A newfound self-assurance and being powerful in new situations.
- The ability to relate to people at a deeper level, not being halted by your assessments, judgments and fears of other people.
- An expanded sense of freedom, satisfaction and peace of mind.
- The ability to clarify and sustain your commitments.
- A newfound enthusiasm for life.

## THE EVOLUTIONS (EXERCISES)

During BUD/S training, the trainees discover within themselves the secrets by performing or undergoing a series of physical exercises called 'evolutions.' There are several evolutions within each day, and they take place over a six-month period. For example, an evolution might be a three-hour run, a five-mile swim or attending a demolition safety procedures class. While physically developing the trainees, a five-mile run also develops within them a number of the secrets simultaneously, such as being steadfast, being an operator and being a teammate. (We'll look at these secrets later on.)

For the sake of your training, each chapter is designed to encompass one secret. At the beginning of each chapter, you are offered insights into the secret, followed by a few evolutions (exercises) at the end. The evolutions give you the opportunity to get the secret experientially. While not physical exercises, the evolutions still require plenty of action on your part.

The idea is to apply them to areas of your life that are currently not working. So, if you are struggling in your career, focus on implementing the evolutions in each chapter that relates to 'career.' The evolutions are essential to your developing yourself as unbeatable in the unworkable areas of your life. They are not to have you DO SEAL missions, but rather to have you develop the perspective or BEING-NESS of a Navy SEAL. The evolutions are designed for you to address issues in your life that your fear may have stopped you from addressing. The idea is not for you to understand the evolutions from an intellectual standpoint or even for you to agree or disagree with them. The idea is for you to DO the evolutions despite your understanding or opinions. Reading about how one learns to swim is far different than jumping off a diving board into unknown water and learning to float, move your body forward and have your breathing in harmony with your body all at the same time. In other words, the only way you'll actually own the secrets, to have them be a part of who you are, is not by understanding them, but by DOING the evolutions. The more diligence you devote to these evolutions, the greater your chance of developing yourself as unbeatable. If you are unwilling to do the evolutions provided in each chapter, there's no need to continue reading this book.

CHAPTER TWO

# The First Secret:
# Be a Volunteer
# (Your Only Other
# Alternative Is to Be
# a Victim)

# Chapter Two

## The First Secret: Be a Volunteer
## (Your Only Other Alternative Is to Be a Victim)

*You don't always get what you want*

—The Rolling Stones

*You always get whut you gel*

—Werner Erhard

*You always get what you tolerate*

—Nancy Zapolski

Navy SEALs are volunteers. They volunteer to undergo six months of rigorous training to demonstrate to themselves, their teammates and the SEAL instructors that they are qualified to further volunteer to put their lives on the line for their personal commitments, their teammates, and for their country.

A volunteer is someone who takes full responsibility for the quality, path and design of his/her life. A victim is someone who blames outside forces, such as the circumstances, bad luck and/or one's parent(s), for the quality, path and design of his/her life. A volunteer is awake or 'present' to the surrounding environment and provides support and positive energy to others. A victim is self-absorbed and drains others of their energy. A volunteer feels blessed for the quality of his/her life, despite obstacles and circumstances. A victim feels victimized by obstacles and circumstances.

(I'm not referring to people who are TRULY victims of outside forces, but those who act as though they are.) Actor and activist, Christopher Reeve, is an example of a classic victim—someone who has EVERY right to feel victimized. The handsome actor is renowned to the world as our movie hero 'Superman.' He had everything that life could offer—his health, a successful career as a talented Hollywood actor, a successful marriage to wife Dana and a healthy family. At an equestrian competition in Culpeper County, Virginia, in 1995, where he was a rider in a cross-country jumping event, Reeve had a horrific accident. The accident occurred on the third jump of a two-mile course. His horse suddenly stopped midway over the fence. Reeve was catapulted headfirst. His fall caused multiple fractures, severing most of the nerves in the spinal bundle that carries signals between his brain and the rest of his body.

I remember watching Reeve during a television interview a few years after the accident. He talked about— and I'm paraphrasing—how difficult his life had become in being paralyzed from the neck down and unable to breathe without a breathing apparatus. For a long time he felt sorry for himself, frustrated and angry. After time and with the support and coaching of his wife, Dana, and others, Reeve began to listen to the outside voices of those who loved him rather than to his own internal dialogue. At some point he gave up BEING victimized, and took on the possibility of transforming the quality of his own life and the lives of others suffering from a wide variety of illnesses and disabilities.

Since the accident, Reeve has not only put a human face on spinal cord injury but he has motivated neuroscientists around the world to conquer the most complex diseases of the brain and central nervous system. In 1999, for example, only four years after the accident, Reeve became the chairman of the board of the Christopher Reeve Paralysis Foundation (CRPF). CRPF is a national, nonprofit organization that supports research to develop effective treatments and a cure for paralysis caused by spinal cord injury and other central nervous system disorders. CRPF also allocates a portion of its resources to grants that improve the quality of life for people with disabilities.

As vice chairman of the National Organization on Disability (N.O.D.), Reeve works on quality of life issues for the disabled. In partnership with Senator Jim Jeffords of Vermont, he helped pass the *1999 Work Incentives Improvement Act,* which allows people with disabilities to return to work and still receive disability benefits. Reeve is also on the Board of Directors of World T.E.A.M. Sports, a group that organizes and sponsors challenging sporting events for athletes with disabilities; TechHealth, a private company that assists in the relationship between patients and their insurance companies; and LIFE or Leaders in Furthering Education, a charitable organization that supports education and opportunities for the underserved population. The list of his ongoing achievements and contributions to others, after the accident, is extraordinary. He writes books, directs movies, continues to act in movies and maintains a rigorous speaking schedule, traveling across the country giving motivational talks to numerous groups, organizations and corporations.

Is this the life of a victim?

The next time your 'baby' walks out on you or cheats on you or you do not get that promotion or you are unable to find the 'zapper' for your television, why don't you try being like Superman?

To be unbeatable is to choose to be a volunteer in your life. This is different than volunteering your time. Being a volunteer in your life is not just for a few hours a week, when you feel like it, or when it is fun, or when you think you understand how the future is going to turn out. Being a volunteer in your life is to understand the basic nature of life: that in every moment you use your free will and choose to be a volunteer or you become victimized by life's circumstances, become reactivated by people's actions, or lack of them, or by their comments and become a victim. Ultimately, your entire life is based on what you choose to be in every moment.

Few people think of themselves as life's volunteer. The *Jerry Springer Show* is but one vivid example of how many people choose to relate to their lives. The audience watches, points fingers and laughs and shouts at the guests, thinking them ridiculous and inferior. (People often laugh when something triggers familiarity or discomfort.) While we make moral judgments about how others act out life's disappointments, the guests' conversations are universal. In each episode, every guest relates to him/herself as a victim. At least one guest per episode rants about giving up his/her life for another person, or going to work for ten hours a day just to please another, or having done EVERYTHING for the other person, only to be left stepped on, cheated on and/or used. People unwittingly relate to themselves as victims rather than being responsible for having had the free will to choose any particular point of view, situation or relationship.

*We have two choices in life—to be a volunteer or to be a victim. Choose!*

The first step in being a volunteer is in discovering those areas where you think and ACT victimized. Victimized people have reasons and justifications to explain their circumstances, such as:

- My father was a jerk.
- My husband controlled me, and I just couldn't get rid of him.
- We were so poor so I never finished high school.
- My mother always put me down and never supported me when I wanted to be a hockey player or doctor. So, I never had the right emotional support to 'make it.'
- I didn't go to the right university.
- I didn't inherit any money like my husband/ wife.
- And on and on and on.

You might not think of yourself as a victim, per se. You might just feel sorry for yourself in a given situation, feel used or feel like you are the good person who is being poorly treated by another. Or, you might think of yourself as the underdog in a particular situation or relationship. Look at those areas of your life where you are unhappy or feel used, trapped, betrayed or controlled by someone else. It is in these areas where you are acting victimized. As far as I can tell, living life as a volunteer is a moment-by-moment process and a lifelong pursuit.

If you are having a difficult time in seeing this, then pick one major area of your life, for example in your career, romantic relationship, family or economic situation. Look to see where you have something or someone other than yourself as responsible for your situation, circumstance and/or condition. For example, are you blaming your ex-spouse for YOUR unhappiness? If in business, are you blaming the fluctuating economy or declining stock market for your inability to produce results? Look to see where your reasons for failing are due to outside events or forces, such as a controlling parent, wife or husband, an unappreciative boss or a lousy economy.

Remember I asked you the question, "Who are you in the matter of your own success?" Whatever word or phrase you came up with is, perhaps, the OBSTACLE that is keeping you from succeeding at your desired level in any area of your life. What you may forget is that YOU created that word or phrase in the first place. When feeling like a failure, such as in love, business and/or career, we tell ourselves reasons and justifications to validate our feelings of defeat. We say things to ourselves, such as, *"I've given up. Business is tough because of the economy."* Then we begin to believe these reasons or justifications (words and/or phrases) as though they are the TRUTH. If we repeat these word and/or phrases to ourselves often enough, they will actually begin to look like the truth, as though they actually exist in reality. We soon come to BELIEVE we are not succeeding because the economy IS tough or our boss IS controlling. Over time, we get to a point where we become victimized by this truth and by our own internal words and/or phrases. The tough economy begins to victimize us.

*You are the creator.*
*Whatever you believe, that is what you create*
*and that is what you become.*
-Gurudev

In each moment you are either being a volunteer (being fully responsible for your life and choices) or you are being a victim (defeated and victimized by your own justifications and reasons.) Anything other than you being fully responsible for all aspects of your life IS a basic lie that you are telling yourself and are most definitely telling others.

The idea of BUD/S training is to take highly qualified volunteers and press them beyond human tolerance. Why? So the instructors could test the trainees' commitment and the resiliency of their spirit—despite their talents, their upbringing, their breaks or lack of breaks in life. I observed several trainees during BUD/S that when the going became difficult—and for each person 'difficult' varied—these trainees succumbed to some inner words and/or phrases, such as, *"I didn't know it was going to be like this!"* They displaced their responsibility for having put themselves in this position in the first place. In these cases, the men then quit as though their reasons, such as not knowing how it would be, superseded their choice and commitment to complete the training. I'm not implying that it is wrong to quit. They did it, and it is long over. Rather than identifying that their reason was but a self-created reason, they bought into the reason as though it was the truth. Then they created a justification for not continuing to volunteer or be in BUD/S of their own free will.

BUD/S is designed to have the trainees discover the relationship between their free will and their commitment. The trainees have the freedom to 'ring the bell' and quit at any time. If they continue, they do so of their own free will . . . and it is painfully obvious. SEALs operate not as victims, not as reactive, but as responsible, active and extraordinary volunteers on a moment-by-moment basis, despite extreme internal and external adversity.

If you are interested in being unbeatable then begin with the expression and acknowledgement of your own free will. It is choosing to be a volunteer every time you find yourself acting like a victim. (If you are presently in a relationship where you feel victimized, consider that you're choosing to be there, when in fact, you could 'ring the bell' at any time.)

By the way, everyone, at one time or another acts victimized by something or someone. It's part of our human-ness. Like everyone, SEALs are not immune to upsets, anger, and annoyance. SEALs complain and engage in self-victimized conversations like everyone else. However, the culture called 'SEAL' has them operate beyond their reasons, rather than indulging in them. A moaning SEAL would find himself in deep *kim chee* if he continued to sing the blues around other SEALs for too long. Other SEALs would quickly deliver a pithy comment to shake the moaner out of it.

---

 *Choosing your commitment moment to moment IS often difficult, no matter what endeavor you choose.*

---

Each choice you make in every moment determines the quality of your life. If the quality of your life is less than you desire, then perhaps you have been relating to most of these choices as though you were a victim rather than as a volunteer.

What if you thought of yourself as life's volunteer? This might mean, for example, you would work fourteen-hour days, mow the lawn, clean the house, make dinner or take the kids to baseball practice—not because you are doing it for your spouse or romantic partner or to keep the peace or to make the other person happy: you would do these things because you willingly choose to do them, despite how much or how little you are appreciated. Period. (When you are a volunteer, you don't need to compare the amount of hard work you're doing to that of another. You just do what needs to be done of your own free will. You may think you are working harder or longer, but the art is in recognizing these victimized thoughts as they come up and simply let them go rather than wallowing in them.)

Imagine the countless arguments you could avoid by simply choosing to be a volunteer in your committed, romantic relationship or in your career. For many, changing jobs and relationships, as a way to fix what is wrong in their lives, while exciting at the outset, quickly becomes a replay of the victim routine. The supporting actors change, but the star of the movie—you—and the screenplay stays the same. As a volunteer, you will experience freedom and satisfaction by admitting to yourself that you are not stuck in a relationship or in a job: that in fact, you choose it of your own free will. This also holds true for your choice of friends, where you live, the state of your financial affairs, and even how you RELATE to your family.

# Evolution for Personal Growth:

Read this chapter again.

**Purpose of Evolution:** To have you let go of your internal conversations of victimization.

**Action:** Write down the person's name who you seem to complain about the most. This might be your romantic partner, your ex-spouse, someone in your family, or someone at work. Under this person's name, write all the reasons as to why you are upset. Here is an example:

Jerry:
He is never on time.
He never calls to say he is going to be late.
He forgets about my birthday.
He takes all that I do for him for granted.
I hate the way he chews his food.
He's sloppy.

Now create another list. Write down all the things you admire about this person. Here is an example:

Jerry:
He is generous to a fault.
He is free spirited and never gets upset.
He loves my family and people in general.
He is funny.
He is creative.
He thinks I'm the best thing that ever happened to him.

Look carefully at both lists. Choose. You can stay in relationship with this person or you can choose to end this relationship. It is YOUR choice.

Every time you hear yourself complaining, choose to be victimized OR choose to give up the complaint and be a volunteer! Share this exercise with your best friend(s). Request that your best friend point out when you are complaining and acting victimized. When you complain, request your best friend stop you midstream and say to you, *"Choose."*

As a volunteer, and if you choose the relationship, negotiate with your boss and/or romantic partner or ex about what you require to have the relationship work.

*Your Insights:*

# CHAPTER THREE

# *The Second Secret: Be Aware (That Your Life Is at Stake!)*

# Chapter Three

## The Second Secret: Be Aware
## (That Your Life Is at Stake!)

*Nothing in life is so exhilarating as to be shot
at without result.*

-Winston Churchill,
The Malakand Field Force, 1898

Why do you suppose Navy SEALs are appreciated, acknowledged, and by many people, honored? It's simple. SEALs put their lives on the line in extraordinary circumstances.

The difference between a Navy SEAL and a lot of other people is that SEALs are aware that their lives are at stake. Everything accomplished is done with this in mind. Their circumstances and actions call for this awareness. Parachuting, diving, working with demolitions, weapons, and running combat missions act as a continuous alarm clock waking them up to reality! When they forget—like cutting corners or thinking they are super-human—the consequences can be fatal.

Being aware that your life is at stake is living in a manner in which you are consciously aware of the consequences of your actions on a moment-by-moment basis. This awareness, this secret, will contribute toward your being unbeatable.

On one operation during my second Vietnam tour, in the middle of the night, my team was patrolling just outside of a village suspected as being a possible Viet Cong (VC) hideout. One of my men suddenly started to exclaim, *"We're surrounded by VC!! We're surrounded by VC!"* Since we were on an island where the VC had been firing B-40 rockets at the U.S. Navy patrol boats, and there were only seven of us, his communication was initially unsettling, to say the least. I told him to shut up; nobody was moving in on us and, if that did happen, I'd be the first to let him know. The patrol continued throughout the night without further incident and no sighting of VC. Had I not been 'wide awake' to reality in that moment, I may have responded to this SEAL's paranoia, ordered the men to open fire and shoot at invisible VC. This would have jeopardized our position and our lives. The point is that many people think that their thoughts or their paranoia—often thought as oneself being intuitive or a good judge of character—IS reality. Reality is, in fact, often contrary to our thoughts. Being aware or 'awake' that your life is at stake is in dealing with reality, not dealing with and/or reacting to or acting out your suspicions or paranoid thoughts. If danger does strike, then you would deal with that reality when it occurs.

Do you know that life offers no security? That security is an illusion? Hard as we try, we have yet to find security from death. One of the truths that SEALs face early on is that life offers no guarantees. SEALS acknowledge that everyone dies and it is only a matter of when. And while a SEAL accepts this, he is also committed to living a full life. This truth keeps SEALS wide awake and aware of reality (what is happening in the universe, not in their heads), and they then live fully in the moment.

*I believe that only one person in a thousand*
*knows the trick of really living in the present.*
*Most of us spend 59 minutes an hour living*
*in the past, with regret and lost joy, or shame*
*for things badly done both utterly useless and*
*weakening—or in a future which we either*
*long for or dread.*
*Yet the past is gone beyond prayer, and every*
*minute you spend in the vain effort to*
*anticipate the future is a moment lost.*
*There is only one world, the world pressing*
*against you at this minute. There is only one*
*minute in which you are alive, this minute—*
*here and now.*
*The only way to live is by accepting each*
*minute as an unrepeatable miracle. Which is*
*exactly what it is—a miracle and*
*unrepeatable.*

-Storm Jameson

There are no guarantees in life. There are no guarantees that your company will prosper or that your job will continue. There are no guarantees that your children will be happy, successful, an asset to society and grow old. There are no guarantees that you will remain healthy or remain married.

*Marriage has no guarantees. If that's what*
*you're looking for, go live with a car battery.*

-Erma Bombeck

For some, this may sound cynical, disheartening or depressing. This truth can have the opposite effect. When you fully understand that your life is at stake, every day will possess richness. It is our illusions and the expectations that our illusions will be fulfilled that cause us to be cynical, disheartened or depressed. For example, when we get married for the first time, we often believe it will last forever. And we all know the current divorce rate. Anyone who has been married and divorced fully understands the difference between the illusion of 'forever' and reality. People create grand illusions and then live as though guarantees are an option and as though the desired outcome is guaranteed. Who said so? We create illusions, get comfortable with them, and then these illusions become invisible to us. Our illusions begin to use and drive us. In response, we live as though life is safe. The murders of John Kennedy, John Lennon and Nicole Simpson and the deaths of Marilyn Monroe, Elvis Presley and Princess Diana leave us disturbed and upset. Why? Because we took for granted that they would be with us until a ripe old age. Their lives, like our own, were never guaranteed.

In watching the news and seeing others suffering, such as parents who lose their children to abduction, we shake our heads in dismay, empathizing with their tragedy—for a moment or two—then change the television channel to a sitcom. Assuming that somebody else or the government will do something, we immediately get back to living in our safe, comfortable and guaranteed illusion—until something dreadful happens to us or to someone in our family or local community! When tragedy strikes, our illusion is shaken, or even shattered. We experience a break in our illusion, or a break in reality. It is not a break, but rather an awakening. We suddenly realize that life was always unsafe. Or we realize that our marriage certificate offered no guarantee or that the boss really didn't care about our seniority when he fired us. For many, this awakening is uncomfortable. They think that they may be cursed with bad luck. It 'ain't' bad luck; it is simply life.

Following all three of my divorces, I needed time to heal. Looking back, I now see that this healing time that I needed after each divorce was really my dealing with the break in my illusion. Each time I believed that THIS marriage would be my last and be FOREVER!

---

 *To be unbeatable is to accept that life is uncomfortable. Let go of your illusions about how life should be and be with what it is.*

---

It is easier and more comfortable to anaesthetize ourselves with alcohol and drugs, mundane activities like watching TV or sharing our opinions about matters from the sidelines.

When you see that your life is at stake, you might notice, in fact, that your worst enemy might be your own mind—your inner self-talk. Self-talk can destroy happiness and kill people slowly. To recognize this, we need only glimpse the lives of Kurt Cobain or Freddie Prince. Successful people can create thick illusions, making them more disillusioned than the rest. Success often provides a powerful and false sense of security—a feeling of invincibility. Success has also been known to cover up a lot of sadness and immaturity. If you look around, you will see some examples in your immediate world, as well as in media reports. If you listen carefully, you might begin to hear your own poisonous self-talk about yourself and about others.

Let us look at how NOT realizing that our lives are at stake ultimately affects the smaller choices we make daily. Have you been late for an appointment? No doubt, more than once. Chances are you have not related to your daily activities as though your life were at stake.

What if your clients' lives were dependent upon you being on time for a meeting or calling them back on the telephone? Right now you are no doubt thinking, *"That's ridiculous! My clients' lives are not at stake, and this has nothing to do with me being on time or calling them back."* The level at which you resist this idea is a sign directly related to the depth of your illusions. You might also want to look at why you are late for appointments. Did you know that being late or not returning phone calls are blatant, albeit indirect, ways for you to 'flip the bird' to others? You are controlling people and/or your environments, all the while pretending like you're not. You pretend as though you are at the mercy of outside forces, like a busy schedule. If you are late for a meeting, for example, everyone in the meeting is affected. Contrary to what you think, your actions reveal to others, on some level, that you are an attention-seeking, willful child. While you may think you are getting away with these things, chances are, people may be disrespecting you and/or gossiping about you behind your back. This is how people behave when they feel as though they are being dishonored. Or worse, others use your tardiness as a justification for their own lack of commitment or performance in a specific area. You think this is a minor thing? So is cancer when it starts out. Being late or not returning phone calls is an indication of a larger issue at work— your unwillingness to observe the etiquette required to truly relate to other people and your inability to see that your life is at stake.

*The simplest way to earn respect and the most powerful way to honor people is to SHOW UP ON TIME!*

What if Navy SEALs related to their word and promises to their teammates during combat in the same way that most of us relate to our romantic partner, family members, friends and work peers?

We think of Navy SEALs as being mentally tough. Mental toughness is not a macho thing. It is a universal attribute. Many powerful women possess mental toughness. It is alluring and attractive! Toughness is the secret that distinguishes the women from the girls. Mental toughness is NOT genetic. Everyone and anyone can be mentally tough.

*Mental toughness is, at the most basic level, keeping your word.*

Keeping your word at a basic level begins with being on time and doing the things that you say you will do. This means keeping your word to yourself and others despite your reasons, justifications and feelings and under ALL circumstances. This includes playing life's game by the rules and not finding a slick way around the rules. This is difficult to do in a world where the media provides evidence of people breaking life's rules in the game they are playing, and then pretending they're not. The news is currently rife with corporate misadventures and collapses based on culprits manipulating or getting around the rules.

In combat, a Navy SEAL's life depends on his teammates keeping their word. Can you imagine how disastrous a U.S. POW rescue mission might be if a SEAL did not keep his word to his teammates, but instead did what he felt was better? Or, if an at-sea rendezvous with a submarine was aborted because one of the SEALs called in to say he felt a bit chilly, thought he was catching a cold or was hung over and wanted to go back to bed?

What would your life be like if you handled your promises and responsibilities like a Navy SEAL? Stop. Take a moment and ask yourself this question again. Now read it slowly to yourself:

*"What would my life be like if I handled my promises and responsibilities like a Navy SEAL?"*

What if you kept your word to yourself and to others as though your life and the lives of your loved ones, teammates, clients, and friends were at stake?

This might mean that if you made a commitment to yourself to go on a diet to lose weight, you would simply lose weight. If you are interested in seeing the level at which you keep your word to yourself with respect to losing weight, take off your clothes and look in the mirror. If you're interested in seeing the level of which you keep your word to others, don't ask yourself, ask the people in your life. That's your reality check!

You might be thinking, *"Well, not EVERYTHING is in my control. What about snowstorms? What about that car accident that kept me from making my appointment on time?"*

What about it? Navy SEALs are trained to work in relationship to the unexpected, although they certainly don't phrase it this way. What is the first lesson a trainee discovers in BUD/S?

*The future is never what you expect. Expectations are an illusion.*

To be unbeatable, you deal with your illusions in the form of contingency plans and procedures to follow in the event of a crisis. This can begin with planning to include extra time to get to meetings on time in case of an unexpected crisis—such as a flat tire or traffic jam. This can also include, for example, choosing a hotel within walking distance of your meetings, so as not to depend on others to drive you or in having to flag down a taxi. This can go as far as choosing a vehicle according to its ability to function in adverse snow conditions rather than in one that has you look 'hip' or 'cool.' To be unbeatable, you will want to relate to your commitments and responsibilities as though you have a lot to do with the way events turn out. You have two choices—keep your word or do NOT keep your word. The choice is yours. The former has you being extraordinary as a matter of routine.

Even with contingency plans, there will be times when things are completely out of your control. When you cannot keep your word, you might acknowledge this failing rather than concealing it. Many people justify their lateness by trying to convince others of how busy they are or how adverse their conditions had become. Did you know that the only person you have convinced of this is yourself? Instead of justifying your lack of action, be gracious enough to simply apologize. When apologizing, you don't need to include your justifications or reasons. Just apologize. In today's world, a powerful apology would have you be extraordinary!

*If you simply keep your word, life becomes simple and organized. Overwhelm and stresses are often the byproducts of unfilled promises.*

Once again, let us stress this whole idea of your life being at stake, and look at this idea from another perspective. Imagine what you could accomplish moment by moment, day after day, if you lived as though your life were at stake. You might be more conscientious about your health—eating well, exercising, visiting the doctor regularly, avoiding or moderating alcohol and drugs, and certainly avoiding alcohol and drugs while driving and while visiting uncertain surroundings. Even with these precautions, life offers no guarantees.

If you were truly awake to the idea that your life is at stake, how would you relate to others? Would you tell people how much you love them? Would you relent, give up your stubbornness and the need to be right about your opinions at all cost and simply apologize? Would you spend more time with your family despite your opinions about them and begin more meaningful conversations about something other than the weather, family gossip or Aunt Gertie's meat loaf? Would you waste precious moments gossiping about others? Would you watch TV night after night?

Here is one of life's many paradoxes: when you live as though your life is at stake and handle everything to do in life with lightning speed—from bringing immediate closure to disagreements with loved ones to handling promises with massive intention—you will no longer feel frantic. You will no longer need anti-depressants and antacids. And you might not need the psychiatrist to listen to your sob stories of self-inflicted victimization, hard luck, and stress and overwhelm.

---

 *When you relate to your life as though your life is at stake, you will experience a sense of certainty, calmness, freedom, and peace of mind IN THE FACE OF chaos, no security and no guarantees in life! Life becomes rich.*

---

## Evolution for Your Romantic Partnership:

Read this chapter again.

**Purpose of Evolution:** To have you relate to your romantic partner as though your lives and the relationship is at stake.

**Action:** For one month do the 'Creating Appreciation Exercise.' The exercise consists of taking time over dinner, and even in front of the children to create a new habit of saying three things that you appreciate about your romantic partner. Ask your children to support you in this exercise by reminding you and your partner to do it if you forget. The exercise can even become a family practice.

*Your Insights:*

---

# Evolution for Family:

Read this chapter again.

**Purpose of Evolution:** To have you live in the moment.

**Action:** On a piece of paper write down the name of the person with whom you have the longest or most heated grudge. Under this person's name, write all the reasons as to why you are holding onto this grudge. Under your reasons, write down what you believe to be this person's point of view of the situation. Be committed to understanding this person's point of view.

CHOOSE to forgive this person. More bluntly, choose to be an adult.

Meet with this person. Tell this person that you have been holding this grudge. Request his/her forgiveness for your pettiness. IT DOES NOT MATTER WHAT YOUR REASONS ARE FOR THIS GRUDGE. They are all B.S. anyway. Remember, your life is at stake.

---

*Your Insights:*

## Evolution for Career:

Read this chapter again.

**Purpose of Evolution:** To have you handle all your commitments as though your life is at stake.

**Action:** For one month show up on time or early for work and keep all your appointments without rescheduling the time of any of them. Whenever you fail at this exercise, write down the primary reason you give yourself for failing. At the end of the month, review what you have accomplished or failed to accomplish.

*Your Insights:*

# CHAPTER FOUR

# *The Third Secret:*
# *Be Yourself*
# *(Your Uniqueness Gets*
# *You into the Game)*

# Chapter Four

## The Third Secret: Be Yourself

## (Your Uniqueness Gets You into the Game)

*At bottom every man knows well enough
that he is a unique being, only once on this
earth; and by no extraordinary chance will
such a marvelously picturesque piece of
diversity in unity as he is, ever be put
together a second time.*

—Friedrich Nietzsche

Being unbeatable includes you daring to be yourself—
EXACTLY AS YOU ARE! You are perfect just the way
you are! You might as well embrace who you are,
because hard as you try, you can never be anyone else,
except an older version of you. Those who try to be
like others are mocked and ridiculed! Those who dare
to be themselves are frequently honored, respected and
admired—Mike Myers, Muhammad Ali, Gilda Radner,
Janis Joplin, Albert Einstein—all come to mind. There
are many others, of course.

To be unbeatable is understanding that you need not change, have more knowledge, be better looking, weigh less or more, etc. (Despite your current weight, you will be a hell of a lot lighter in 150 years!) To think you can significantly change who you are—at a core level—is as insane as thinking that a new haircut will make you a new person.

Sometimes, within a declining romantic relationship one partner will begin to panic, believing he/she must CHANGE to have the relationship work. This is the recipe for disaster. If you really accepted that you are perfect just the way you are, you would not have to change yourself or have any need to get better just to have your relationship work. Trying to change yourself only reinforces who you already are. The old French adage, 'The more things change, the more they stay the same,' applies. Besides, changing yourself is not a prerequisite to being unbeatable, or, for that matter, recreating your life as extraordinary. You are already perfect—even with what you consider your character flaws.

> *I'm basically a sexless geek. Look at me,*
> *I have pasty-white skin, I have acne scars*
> *and I'm five-foot-nothing. Does that sound*
> *like a real sexual dynamo to you?*
>
> -Mike Myers

Why not embrace your uniqueness and recreate your life from there? Why not focus on recreating yourself, your life instead of trying to change it all? I do not mean that you are free from mistakes, failings or character flaws. When a female lion goes hunting for food, she doesn't, on those occasions when her stalk and charge come up empty, berate herself for having failed! Can you imagine another lion saying, *"Jeez, Elsa, you pounced a little too soon on that gnu,"* or, *"I think you need some anger management, Elsa, 'cause your judgment is affecting your pounces."* That is part of the lioness's perfection. The lioness's perfection is that she immediately corrects her behavior without entertaining conversations about failure. A wildlife documentarian might say the lioness made a mistake, but not the lioness. The lioness continues to hunt. The lioness is perfect!

---

*Only human beings come up with failure as an explanation about an action that produced less than the desired result. Your perfection includes the failures you or others assign!*

---

*Who is it that says most?*
*Which can say more*
*than this rich phrase—that you alone are*
*you?*

—William Shakespeare

---

*By embracing your perfection, you are qualifying yourself to participate in your own life.*

---

My fellow BUD/S trainees were, for the most part, content with themselves. They set about acquiring the skills necessary for the game they were playing, for example, preparation for and participation in combat, and they pursued these skills exactly as themselves. In other words, the funny guys maintained their humor; the serious guys, their seriousness. As disciplined and unbeatable as they were, the trainees were also individualistic . . . a definite strength.

Recreating your life as extraordinary is NOT about changing yourself. You don't have to WORK at changing yourself because you're always changing whether you want to or not. Change is inevitable. Every day we grow older. We change emotionally, intellectually, spiritually and definitely physically on a moment-by-moment basis throughout our lifetime. So, you don't have to WORK HARD or TRY to change who you are because it happens naturally. You might argue that you NEED to change because there are qualities about you that just don't work for you and/or for others in your life. This perception reveals that you fundamentally believe that there is something wrong with you that needs to be changed or fixed. The problem is if you try to change these negative behaviors, you will only be reinforcing their existence. It is like deciding to go on a diet only to realize that you spend most of your time thinking about food until you finally relent, eat everything in sight, and end up weighing more than you did before the diet.

YOU ARE NOT YOUR BEHAVOIRS. People often collapse these ideas. You might do something that is not workable, consider it to be a 'bad' behavior, and then tell yourself and others that you need to change, or that you are a bad person, or that you don't like yourself. If you believe that you are perfect just the way that you are, and that your unworkable behaviors are not who you are, then it's much easier to simply let go of the behaviors that no longer work. People spend far too much time and energy resisting or hiding their own human-ness. Another way to say this is that we have darkness—the human side—and we have light—the 'being' side. While living on this planet, we will always be a whole HUMAN BEING (darkness and light).

*Trying to change yourself is like trying to get rid of your darkness, which is trying to be something other than human. Good Luck.*

To be unbeatable is you accepting yourself exactly as you are in all your darkness and your light. It is to be responsible for your darkness so as to not hurt yourself and others, and then dare to recreate your life as extraordinary, including you being yourself.

In BUD/S, there were trainees who dared to be themselves, despite being ridiculed from other trainees and the instructors. In BUD/S, in 1964, we had a short, skinny trainee in our group who looked like an oversized ferret and who ran like Jiminy Cricket! Before you become outraged at my callous description, remember, beauty (or ferret) is in the eye of the beholder! Besides, we all had nicknames. My fellow trainees called me 'turtle' because I smoked two packs of unfiltered Camels a day and ran as one might expect. In BUD/S we laughed at each other and quickly learned to laugh at ourselves.

When running, the group moved together in a steady rhythm, like we were on cruise control. This kept our minds off the pain and the instructor's constant 'encouragement.' Jiminy Cricket, on the other hand, ran with quick, teeny-tiny footsteps. At the time I thought to myself, *"Jiminy ain't no frogman."* I hated running behind him; I quickly lost rhythm with the group as my attention was on Jiminy. Jiminy annoyed the hell out of me, or at least I thought so at the time. On more than one occasion, I yelled at him to move to the back of the group or run like the rest. Jiminy was impervious to my ridicule. He ran at his own pace, smiling the whole time. His carefree attitude REALLY annoyed the hell out of me, as I was in agony. By the end of the training, I discovered that our scuttling friend was consistently in the top group of runners, AND he never appeared to be experiencing stress or pain. Jiminy was renowned for his ability to run all day. I ended up being one of the over all slowest runners in my class. Despite the constant ridicule and heckling, the repeated adversity, Jiminy WAS unbeatable. In other words, his running ability made him unique in BUD/S. But it was his unbeatable attitude in the face of all the adversity that had him stand out as extraordinary.

---

 *Your talent makes you unique, not extraordinary. It is the way in which you handle yourself beyond your talent and the way in which you relate to your life and to others that has you be extraordinary.*

---

You might argue with my premise on change and still want to change to 'be a better you,' as though you plan to be somehow different in the future. That's fine. However, being unbeatable is an ATTITUDE that you CHOOSE to possess on a MOMENT-BY-MOMENT basis throughout your lifetime.

It is not a goal to work toward. In every moment, you have the choice: call yourself a failure or accept the failing and move beyond it. That is . . . be like the lioness.

Life gets dicey when we fail repeatedly. After failing, it takes time, sometimes plenty of time, to recover, if we recover at all. Failing can wear away at our inspiration and motivation and seem to get replaced with feelings of fatigue, defeat and low self-esteem. That is why, to be unbeatable, you RE-create your life as extraordinary the second after you fail. What does it mean to RE-create your life? It means that you acknowledge that your fatigue and defeat comes from the rationalizations and reasons you have as to why you failed. These justifications are always self-defeating. In the face of failing, I'm sure you have heard yourself say something on the order of, *"I'm no good. I'm a loser. I'm not talented. I'm not good enough."* Or you might also say, *"I didn't want that position, anyway. It wasn't meant to be. The timing was off. If only the economy had turned for the better."* We create these justifications because our lives are unconsciously run by a much younger 'us,' our inner child, if you will. It is our unfulfilled childish expectations that leave us tired and defeated, NOT the failings themselves. In accepting this, you have the opportunity to begin anew, IN THE MOMENT, without holding onto your past. Herein lies the sense of freedom that allows you to recreate your life, to be unbeatable and to live extraordinarily.

---

*There is a DIRECT relationship between the number of times one fails and the size or capacity of the accomplishment. The greater the accomplishment, the more one can expect to fail to achieve it!*

---

When Michael Jordan played for the Chicago Bulls and would miss a shot, he refrained from nose diving and indulging in thoughts of failure. He stayed focused on the outcome of the game—his ultimate goal. With each shot he began anew, as though it was his first. He avoided bringing the history of past shots—good or bad—into his awareness when he played. He literally recreated himself moment by moment. Practicing his whole life, Michael Jordan continued to thrive in the face of his own self-defeating thoughts and repeated failings by playing his particular game full out.

Once YOU have a game or goal worthy of your commitment, you can play full out, fail repeatedly, and get mentoring or coaching on your weak points and play full out again. If you are saying to yourself, *"I don't have any weak points,"* then you don't need a coach—you need a couch! And you certainly don't need this book. Instead, open a bag of potato chips and enjoy being an armchair jockey preaching to others on how to play the game of life.

Honor yourself and take pride in your uniqueness. In the face of failing, look objectively at your weak areas and then begin ANEW! All this happens moment to moment.

You don't need to change to be different sometime in the future. There is no place to get to in life. There is only now. Life is happening right now . . . right now . . . and right now. Life IS this moment.

---

 *To be unbeatable is an attitude you choose NOW and continue to choose moment by moment throughout your life.*

---

---

### Evolution for Your Romantic Partnership:

Read this chapter again.

**Purpose of Evolution:** To have you be yourself within your romantic partnership.

**Action:** Once a week for a month, share with your partner a secret that you have kept to yourself for fear of him/her judging and/or assessing you. This can be something from your past and/or something you fantasize about. Be responsible when communicating your fantasies. Remember, they ARE fantasies, not expectations to set upon your partner.

---

*Your Insights:*

# Evolution for Family:

Read this chapter again.

**Purpose of Evolution:** To expand your self-expression and embrace your uniqueness.

**Action:** On the top of a piece of paper, write your name and underline it. Under your name, make a list of the people with whom you have withheld saying what you are thinking or feeling, such as resentments toward them, acknowledgements about them, requests that you have of them, etc. Specify for each person why you have not said what you have wanted to say that might otherwise have you being in relationship with him or her. (I'm not talking about going-through-the-motion pleasantries! I'm talking about truly being related.) Also, write down your reasons/justifications for not communicating. Then ask yourself the question, *"Am I willing to be myself, be expressed and in relationship with this person?"* If the answer is yes, communicate. (If the answer is no, continue to suffer, be suppressed, withheld, etc., and let another relationship slip by you.) If this person is upset or annoyed after you communicate, then you have probably cast blame, maybe not 'blame' in your words, but certainly in the way you are behaving. Be responsible for your perceptions and the way in which you communicate to others. Do the evolution again.

In communicating resentments, be clear that your resentment has nothing to do with what the other person did or did not do. Your resentments are based on YOUR expectations—your thoughts about what the other person should, shouldn't, could have or could not have done—in other words, your expectations for which YOU

ALONE are responsible. It is no one's job in life to live up to your expectations. For example, you might say,

> *"Jerry, I've resented you for not giving me that promotion. I thought that you should have given it to me. I've re-thought it and I now realize that you alone are/were in a position to determine who gets promoted. I've given up my resentment towards you, and I apologize for not playing full out in my job. What can I do to turn this around?"*

Feel uncomfortable with the idea of this communication? Good.

## *Your Insights:*

## Evolution for Career:

Read this chapter again.

**Purpose of Evolution:** To have you be confident with your own uniqueness at work and with people you do not know.

**Action:** Choose three people that you do not know and with whom you have no ulterior motive, such as angling for a promotion or a romantic date. Over a one-week period, introduce yourself to these people.

*Your Insights:*

# CHAPTER FIVE

# *The Fourth Secret: Be Disciplined (Willing to Be, as You Have Never Been Before)*

# Chapter Five

## The Fourth Secret: Be Disciplined

## (Willing to Be, as You Have Never Been Before)

*Discipline is the soul of an Army.*
*It makes small numbers formidable, procures*
*success to the weak, and esteem to all.*

—George Washington
(Letter of Instructions to the Captains of
the Virginia Regiments, July 29, 1759)

As odd as this sounds, reading this book, alone, will make little difference for you in your life. Reading is but a starting point to recreate your life as extraordinary. Books are an escape, just like a game of golf, a fine cigar, a delicious glass of wine or a great workout. Books provide people with hope that their lives might be different. Reading a book on how to play golf or on how to discern the subtle qualities of a Cabernet from a Merlot will give you information. Information alone rarely makes a difference. It can have an impact, but you, the reader—not the author and usually when the timing is just right—determine this. SEALs do not read books to learn how to BE SEALs. They learn through practice and experience, failing over and over and over again. (Easier said than done.) It will take courage for you to put these evolutions into practice. To do this, you will have to be an 'operator.' (This is a SEAL secret that will be fully expressed later on.) For now, suffice to say that to be unbeatable, you must train yourself to be disciplined.

When entering BUD/S, the trainee is taught discipline. It is unnatural. We don't wake up in the morning being disciplined. Discipline is not like having blue eyes and brown hair. In other words, it's not genetic.

What is discipline? It is YOU willing to have an attitude to be highly trainable in whatever you choose to do. The key word here is trainable. Navy SEALs are trained to be HIGHLY TRAINABLE volunteers. In BUD/S they choose, of their own free will, to be trained by their teammates and the SEAL instructors, even though they have no idea what's going to happen in the upcoming six months! In other words, they WILLINGLY chose to be open to EVERYTHING and ANYTHING others are offering and view this information, not as advice or criticism, but as a genuine contribution toward their personal success. When others offer you advice, even unsolicited advice, how do you interpret it?

In the beginning of BUD/S, most of us resisted listening effectively and taking directions from the instructors. Our rebellion was rarely verbalized because we were not stupid! Our resistance showed up as us going through the motions on certain activities—being 'checked out' so to speak. Some trainees liked to overdramatize their aches and pains—unless it was an activity in which they were proficient. When the class dragged butt, the instructors had us do a simple activity over and over and over again. We were being trained to have a highly trainable attitude.

*W'en ol man Rabbit say 'scoot,' dey scooted, en
w'en ol Miss Rabbit say 'scat,' dey scatted.*

-Joel Chandler Harris (Uncle Remus
and His Friends, 1892)

In BUD/S, we rarely rode anywhere . . . we ran. One time, however, for training in hydrographic reconnaissance, we rode on a large six-by-six Army truck from our barracks to the beach. We carried our survey equipment (steel poles attached to plywood squares, reels with lines, etc.,) plus personal swim gear. The load was awkward and cumbersome to carry and take off the truck. The first few times we did this exercise, the instructors disliked our tardiness and disorganization. We took our time, carefully removing the equipment. As a result, the instructors had us do an evolution called, 'On the Truck/Off the Truck.' This consisted of everyone repeatedly getting on the truck and off the truck (with all of our equipment) at the instructor's command and as RAPIDLY as possible, over and over and over again. It looked like mass confusion and seemed purposeless to us at the time. A scene from the movie, *Cool Hand Luke,* starring Paul Newman as Luke, captured the essence of this idea. In one scene, Luke was ordered by one guard to dig a hole, and after hours of work, was told by another outraged guard to fill the hole, over and over again.

The next time we rode the truck to the beach, our class conspired to get off the truck before the order, *"Off the truck!"* was called out. We also pre-assigned the duties for each man ahead of time. We were ready! When the instructor yelled, *"Off the . . ."*

We exploded out of that vehicle like a demolition charge had been placed under our butts. The trainees yelled, *"Hooooo Yahhhhhh!"* It was pandemonium! We were off that truck, with gear in hand, and down to the beach in three seconds. The instructors ordered us to stop and to get back into formation. One of the instructors, Tom Blais, walked up and down in front of the formation, lavishing praise on us that we had never before heard during our training. He went on and on about how much spirit we demonstrated. He said, *"I've never seen a class with SO MUCH enthusiasm."* In finishing, he said to the second instructor standing in back, *"Bernie, is there anything you would like to say to these men?"* Instructor Bernie Waddell said, *"Why, yes, Tom, there is something I would like to say. There is something I would like to say. Class I would like to say something."* (Waddell always repeated things three times.) *"And what I would like to say is this . . . YOU ALL STINK! THAT STUNK! THAT WAS DISGUSTING! THAT'S THE MOST DISGUSTING DISPLAY I'VE SEEN IN ALL MY LIFE. IT WAS REALLY DISGUSTING AND STUNK!"* Waddell went on like this for five minutes. I personally thought this rant was as funny as hell. I am unsure as to what the other guys were thinking. Instructor Tom Blais finished by saying, *"Well, since we have a disagreement, I'll have to go with Bernie's assessment. So, you are all going for a run."*

We were ordered to run in the soft sand until the end of the day. Over time and with much repetition, adversity and pain, we learned to LISTEN as though we had antennae implanted in our ears. We quickly learned the meaning of discipline. In other words, we were becoming highly trainable volunteers.

Navy SEALs, due to their extensive training in BUD/S, choose to listen to the instructors as mentors and choose to possess an attitude to be highly trainable. They would never think of Frank Sinatra's song, 'My Way,' as their SEAL anthem!

Feel confronted by this thought? Do you feel

confronted by the idea of someone, like your romantic partner or your boss, being your mentor? Are you confronted by the idea of doing things someone else's way rather than your own? If you've been doing things 'your way' in one area of your life, such as in owning your business, and you are highly successful, then there is no need to alter what is already working for you—IN THAT AREA. But remember, the more successful you are, the greater your justification to hold on to your limited point of view. Often our greatest attribute in one area of our life can be our biggest curse in another. If you are successful in business, for example, how successful are you in other areas of your life, such as with your relationship to your father or mother or with your romantic partner? Everyone has area(s) in their lives that simply do not work. You might want to consider giving up the idea of doing things your way in these less than satisfying areas. BE TRAINABLE! In these areas, you might want to ask others, such as your romantic partner, family members or teammates, if your headstrong attitude has interfered with or thwarted your relationship with them. In the game called BUD/S, the trainees know that doing things their way would guarantee one thing—mediocre results. Being highly trainable is to give up the notion that everything has to go your way. It's not what you do. It is an attitude you choose to possess.

If you resist this idea and insist on doing things your way, even in the areas of your life that don't work, be aware that you will continue to experience predictable reactions and few, if any, results. If you keep in mind that you are merely acting like a gerbil on a wheel, you can find joy in knowing you are going nowhere.

Furthermore, if you are someone who prides yourself in doing things your way, I also ask you to think about this: your way is nothing more than the combined contributions of many people, in the form of your DNA, language, cultural background, environment, family, religion, and childhood that unconsciously shape the choices and decisions you make on your own. Thinking that you have been doing it your way ignores the contributions many others have generously and graciously made to you. Believing you are solely responsible for your successes is arrogant and delusional. Thinking that you are the only true rebel is ordinary! Everyone thinks they are some sort of a rebel. Just consider it, Bunky.*

*People seldom improve when they have no other model but themselves to copy after.*

—Oliver Goldsmith

SEALs are among one of many extraordinary groups of individuals who are trainable in ways that others have tested and proved workable. Other groups that similarly take on training include top ranked athletes, musicians, teachers, medical professionals, etc.

---

 *The most successful people in the world are the most trainable.*

---

So upon finishing this book, consider taking on a new level of discipline by finding yourself a mentor or coach. Choose someone you trust to hold you accountable to your commitments. This must be someone who has the

---

\*   *'Bunky' is a name used by young campers for their roommate(s) and is short form for 'bunkmate.'*

courage to talk 'straight' and keep you aligned with YOUR commitment. A purely sympathetic mentor is no mentor at all. A powerful mentor keeps you accountable despite your reasoning! A great mentor is committed to your greatness and calls you to action. (You might want to find yourself a mentor who will hold you accountable to fulfilling the evolutions in this book.)

*A coach is someone who tells you what you don't want to hear, and has you see what you don't want to see so you can be who you have always known you could be.*

—Tom Landry,
Former Dallas Cowboy's coach

Obtaining a mentor or coach is one way you commit to being unbeatable, in being trainable in a specific area of your life, such as in business, a romantic relationship, or in your relationship to your family. Many think that obtaining a mentor or coach is enough. It isn't. It's but one part of the equation. The other part, the most important part, is in you committing to be disciplined or trainable. In AA or Alcoholics Anonymous, alcoholics take on a sponsor, who acts like a coach per se, supporting them to keep their promise to stay sober. (AA has an incredibly high success rate!)

*Personally I'm always ready to learn, although I do not always like being taught.*

—Winston Churchill

To be trainable means to get out of your own way—getting outside your rock-hard points of view. It is to possess the willingness for others to contribute to you and allowing them to do so. I am sure you have participated in someone else's success without having had the formal title of mentor or coach. If so, then you can relate to the satisfaction a mentor experiences when another achieves his/her goals.

I've heard people pride themselves on doing it alone. Nature dictates that TWO people create life. It also takes AT LEAST two people to recreate one person as extraordinary! Just ask Dr. Phil. He may be a hell of a therapist, but he looks great on TV because of his wife's great taste in clothes! In other words, even Dr. Phil—a world-class teacher—lets his wife mentor him about certain things.

Trainable people trust their mentors. SEALs possess an unfaltering trust toward their shipmates. Not blind trust. People make mistakes; therefore, so do SEALs. We all unknowingly filter the advice we will or will not accept from others by virtue of our point of view. We often think our point of view is the 'truth' or the right way. So we refuse to trust another person's point of view and refuse to try doing things their way. Being trainable is accepting all the knowledge your mentor is willing to offer whether you agree with it or not. Complete trust, coupled with straight communication, builds excellence. Without it, you are wasting your time in obtaining a mentor. Speaking of trust, you may want to look at the depth to which you distrust people in all areas of your life.

In the 1970s I had the privilege of working with officers from the Los Angeles Police Department (LAPD). One of the officers told me about the three stages of life for a police officer. He said, *"When you first join the force, you are eager and excited, and discover that there are three groups of people—the police officers, the general public, and the assholes (criminals.) After ten years, you gradually realize that there are only two groups of people, the officers and the assholes (everyone other than the police.) After fifteen years on the force, you realize that there is you and everyone else is an asshole!"*

I'm not representing that this is the attitude of all in the LAPD, but certainly the attitude possessed by the one with whom I spoke. This is but one example of how we all, over time, become deeply distrustful. What is the depth to which you distrust people? You are going to have to look at this if you chose to obtain a mentor or coach.

Obtaining a mentor in an area where you are committed to something is a great idea. However, what is the degree to which you are invested in your commitment? If you are at a stage, such as, *"I'll do my best for as long as I like it,"* then consider that you are untrainable at least at this particular time in your life.

Until your life is about your commitments, you will be wasting your time in obtaining a mentor!

To be trainable is listening powerfully, to the details, without argument. In essence, you have committed yourself to listen to another person's point of view— one you CHOSE of your own free will. Notice if your self-talk obstructs your listening. People assess and judge everything others say. It is part of being human. Start to be aware of your constant assessments.

Along with listening, be sure to implement the training. Trainable people do their assignments AND go beyond what their mentor requests. Remember, it's an attitude. So, if your boss suggests you hone specific skills, you willingly obtain additional training outside the office—that is trainability! If, at Weight Watchers, you are asked to exercise for 35 minutes a day, you do it.

What might your romantic relationship look like if you adopted the idea that your partner could be a mentor to you? And vice versa? Being trainable is in going beyond what your partner requests of you. It is an attitude. If your partner suggests you place the dishes in the dishwasher in a more logical way, you do it AND look for ways to use your partner's logic in cleaning other areas of the house. This is not done to make the other person happy, but for YOU to take on having an unbeatable attitude. One partner, it seems, always demands a higher level of cleanliness in the house than the other. I'm not talking about those neurotic individuals who are obsessed by conquering the intangible idea of perfection. I am talking about those who have a healthy commitment to excellence. (BUD/S training develops, in the trainee, an attitude of impeccability.) The lazy partner usually thinks of him/herself as relaxed, able to go with the flow, etc. If you're the relaxed one, the perfect defense is for you to call your fastidious partner 'anal retentive.' (One of my ex-wives once called me 'anal retentive' when I was going over my monthly bank statement so as to balance it to the penny. At the time I didn't know what the term meant exactly. But with the words 'anal' and 'retentive' in one phrase, I figured it wasn't high praise for my math abilities. She had a habit, despite the amount of money she made, of never knowing her checkbook balance and so bounced many checks accompanied by penalty fees. I thanked her for the compliment and told her she might like to work toward a little retentiveness herself.)

Back to the topic of cleanliness, the cycle begins, day after day, year after year with this issue left unresolved. If your partner demands a higher level of cleanliness, be trainable and commit to learn the details. What do you have to lose? Other than the relationship! To be trainable is to stop defending yourself and consider that perhaps your partner is not anal, but instead possesses a high level of integrity in the cleaning department and a healthy commitment to excellence. Based on my training in BUD/S, I can promise you that the more committed you become to keeping your living quarters impeccable and yourself physically fit, the more freedom and peace of mind you will experience—not to mention physical health. I once heard a guru from India say that the state of one's closet is the state of one's soul. What is the state of your closets? Could you be this trainable? Could you accept your romantic partner as a mentor? Chances are you would rather argue, get upset, blame your partner for whatever is amiss, feel picked on, defeated or resigned or deliberately do the opposite saying, *"NO ONE IS GOING TO CONTROL ME!"* Can you hear the kid's voice in that statement? Keep in mind that your willingness to have a trainable attitude and be trained by your partner will go a LONG WAY in having your partner gladly and willingly meet YOUR needs and requests.

As an aside, no one is ever controlling or TRYING to control you no matter how many people agree with your 'truth.' If someone tells you to do something, you either do it or you don't. Either way, your CHOICE is your responsibility. No one can control you! If you think they can, or that they have been trying to do this, then consider that you are acting victimized and blaming the other person for your inability to be responsible for your own choice and to be responsible for the state of your life.

To be trainable means to be fully responsible for your choice to be trained. You will know when you are acting victimized; you will hear yourself saying things, such as, *"I HAVE TO do what the boss said"* or *"I NEED to do what my wife said"* or *"My husband is MAKING ME do a certain thing."* The moment you are willing and FULLY responsible for your own choice to be trained, you will be honing the secret called 'discipline.'

When around others, acknowledge your mentor. Trainable people honor their mentors, as SEALs honor their shipmates. During the Oscar Awards, have you noticed how the winners ALWAYS acknowledge those who have contributed toward their success? (As an aside, if you're in business for yourself when was the last time you telephoned your clients and thanked them for their contribution toward your success? Or your banker? I'm not talking about sending a Christmas card or hosting a client appreciation event. I'm referring to a personal phone call.)

---

*To be trainable is in recognizing that victory in any area of life takes a minimum of a 'Dynamic Duo.'*

---

Trainability or discipline goes beyond the action of getting trained or in being trainable. It is a perspective one has moment by moment throughout life. You can get to a place in life where everyone in your life is your mentor—even strangers and children. Numerous times I've been stuck in behaving a certain way or doing something that just didn't work. I was unaware that things were not working until someone I loved, such as one of my five children, pointed it out to me—either through their reactions or by telling me directly. It has taken years of personal training and having others train me to get to a place where I am willing to allow others, including my children, to contribute to me. How often are we open enough to allow our children to train us about life?

When my son Christopher was a young boy, I often took him to the local barbershop for our haircuts. The barbers seemed macho—at least by outward appearances. Hunting trophies adorned their walls, and

*Guns and Ammo* magazines were stacked on their waiting room table. They talked the manly talk. When business was slow they frequented the bar next door to down a boilermaker or two.

These barbers kept a big tub of bubble gum and lollypops in a cabinet under the sink for the kids. After each haircut, one of the barbers would give Christopher a choice between a lollypop and a piece of gum. One time, instead of waiting for the barber, Christopher headed straight for the cabinet, reached in and pulled out a lollypop. Starting for the door, he suddenly turned around and went back to the tub to get a second one. Handing it to me he said, *"Here, Dad, this is for you."* I momentarily stopped, pretended to be appreciative and took the lollypop. As I did, I thought, *"What are these guys going to think of me if I accept this lollypop? That I'm some . . . wienie?"* So, as Christopher walked out the door, I quickly turned back and threw the lollypop back into the tub, making sure the barbers noticed. Christopher and I started down the sidewalk. My son was sucking on his lollypop, when he turned to me and said, *"Where's your lollypop, Dad?"* I frowned and shook my head. *"That's alright, Christopher,"* I said. *"I don't eat lollypops."* Christopher's face and eyes filled with hurt. In that moment I felt ashamed. I realized that my image was more important to me than allowing my son to make a contribution to me. Looking down at my son I said, *"Christopher, I made a mistake."* I returned to the barbershop, went straight to the tub and took out a lollypop. I held it up to show the barbers that I had it—as though I were suddenly proud of the fact. I went outside, opened the wrapper and stuck the sucker into my mouth. Christopher beamed.

Today, as I look back, I can say that had I not seen myself through responding to my son's disappointment,

I would have missed out on one of the fondest memories of my relationship with him. Being connected with those I love is far more important than protecting my false sense of identity or ego, certainly more rewarding than my need to be right about anything, including my idea of how a real man should behave. By being trainable—which is a moment-by-moment process—you can get to a place in life where ALL advice, including that from your kids, is considered as great training.

# Evolution for Your Romantic Partnership:

Read this chapter again.

**Purpose of Evolution:** To have your romantic partner be your mentor.

**Action:** What is your partner's greatest complaint about you? For example, is your partner annoyed by your frequent lateness? Does your partner say that you're cleaning impaired? Are you frequently grumpy? Do you spend too little time with the family? What is your partner's greatest complaint about you?

Have your partner be your mentor and train you in the area of your weakness instead of you being the usual defensive you. While getting the training, listen to all advice and/or criticism from your partner as a contribution toward the success of your relationship. As difficult as this is, implement the training and remember that you're a VOLUNTEER NOT A VICTIM! Conversations like, *"No man/woman is going to CONTROL me!"* or *"You can't tell me what to do!"* or *"You have more problems than I do, so you have no right to be my mentor,"* reveals your inability to be trainable.

If this conversation ends up in an argument, consider that you are responsible for the tension as you are STILL BEING UNTRAINABLE.

Remember, you are the one reading this book, which means YOU'RE the one who is to implement the training from your partner. YOU'RE NOT THE MENTOR! If you use this material to continue to 'try to' control your romantic partner in the name of being a mentor, remember you're not one. In polite terms, you're an arrogant bully.

## *Your Insights:*

# Evolution for Family:

Read this chapter again.

**Purpose of Evolution:** To have you be trainable with respect to your parents' advice.

**Action:** Find an area of your life in which your parents have been nagging you and/or trying to offer you advice. (It doesn't matter how old you are, either.) Take their advice as 'training' and implement it. Also let your parents know that you have done this. Next, apologize to them for resisting their input (if you have) and acknowledge them for their continued concern and love for you. If you cannot get past your 'truth' that your parents are criticizing or controlling you, consider you are still untrainable. Keep doing this evolution until you succeed.

*Your Insights:*

## Evolution for Career:

Read this chapter again.

**Purpose of Evolution:** To have you obtain a mentor in an area of your career where you are committed to succeeding but are PRESENTLY FAILING.

**Action:** Ask yourself the question, *"Is this area worth me giving everything I have (my life) toward it?"* If the answer is *'no,'* find an area that is worth you giving your time and energy to pursue. If you fail to find an area, consider that you are being undisciplined and untrainable, and just be happy with small successes. If you find an area to which you can be committed, find yourself a mentor who specializes in this particular field. This may be in the realm of learning a new computer program, polishing your writing skills, getting a college degree, etc. It is unnecessary for you to have the warm and fuzzies for your mentor. In fact, the degree to which you 'like' your mentor is INVERSELY PROPORTIONAL to the level of results you achieve. You CAN respect and admire your mentor . . . but if you 'like' the mentor, chances are the mentor is not pressing you beyond your self-imposed limits.

*Your Insights:*

# CHAPTER SIX

## *The Fifth Secret: Be Willing to Fail (As Part of Your Success)*

# Chapter Six

## The Fifth Secret: Be Willing to Fail

## (As Part of Your Success)

*Success is moving from failure to failure
without any loss of enthusiasm.*

—Winston Churchill

Many people become dramatic when they fail. They conjure up legitimate reasons to quit and then convince themselves that their imaginings are the TRUTH. After all, reasons are logical, rational, justifiable and always COMFORTABLE. When was the last time you heard words like *logical, rational, justifiable and comfortable* alongside words like *excellence, brilliance, creativity, possibility and extraordinary?*

Failing is different from failure. Failing is being unsuccessful at something. You can always attempt it again . . . and again. Failing is growth and movement. You could call it 'the art of failing to succeed.' Being a failure, however, is a decision you make about yourself, a decision based on your justifications, a decision you relate to as a FACT. *"I am a failure."* It is definitive, an ending, with no room for movement, growth or success. To be unbeatable is to become a master of failing. BUT, you will never BE a failure—unless YOU say so. Shaquille O'Neal, arguably one of the finest professional basketball players today, devotes extra time to his weakness (free-throw shooting) for which he had been ridiculed by sportswriters and fans. He obtained the services of a coach to improve this specific skill. The media now respects his free-throw shooting.

As a completely unnecessary aside, when was the last time you saw a sportswriter shooting free-throws for the money?

SEALs are masters of failing. Said another way, extraordinary people relate to the world as though 'everything is possible' and so keep going despite repeated failings. In each moment that you fail, you recognize your reasons for failing, let go of them, recreate yourself and your life, and then generate the missing secrets. In other words, refrain from upsetting yourself by listening and believing your own point of view as to why you failed. Ignore the reasons you tell yourself. Mastering the art of failing is in shortening the recovery time you need to wallow before attempting your goal again. Failing at the level of Navy SEAL is to be at 'one,' in union with your commitment so much so that you require NO recovery time between failings.

*The usual masculine disillusionment is discovering that a woman has a brain.*

—Margaret Mitchell
(*Gone With The Wind*, 1936)

I have been a SEAL in my romantic life—that is to say I have mastered the art of failing! I've been married and divorced three times. While leading seminars around the world, participants asked me about my background. When I mentioned that I had three failed marriages, the audiences would gasp. Their faces revealed, *"There must be something wrong with this guy."* or *"No one in his right mind would be stupid enough to marry and divorce THREE times!"* or *"No woman in her right mind would date this guy."* Some participants stood up and verbalized their opinions. I would have said the same thing. With each marriage, I vowed 'Until death do us part.' In reality my commitment amounted to: 'Until either of us couldn't stand it any longer.' The first time, I married a beautiful brunette who was grounded and religious. Her name was Diane, and she blessed me with two beautiful, intelligent and loving girls, Kim and Amy. In one incident when I was age thirty, and while we were on a trial separation, Diane contacted a Navy chaplain to counsel me. The first time I knew she had done this was when I received a call in my office on the Navy base from this chaplain. At that time, I was the commanding officer of an Underwater Demolition Team and was quietly proud of this achievement. The chaplain did most of the talking.

After an hour, and based on whatever my mumbling responses had been, the chaplain said, *"Jack, you are the coldest person I have ever talked to."* I distinctly remember thinking of how proud I was of this assessment. It was just about the highest compliment anyone could have paid me . . . at that time.

> *You are young, my son, and, as the years go*
> *by, time will change and even reverse many*
> *of your present opinions.*
> *Refrain therefore a while from setting yourself*
> *up as a judge of the highest matters.*

> —Plato (Laws)

Little did I realize that my talent for swimming didn't extend to my romantic life, which was beginning to sink. Diane had not yet realized she had ended up with a boy in a man's body who had completely shut down his emotions as a way to deal with his job. Neither did I! I actually believed I was a man. She didn't know because I refused to communicate or to consider that I was anything less than great! In considering my behavior much later, I saw that I had been an arrogant, insensitive kid, intent only on his job and ill-prepared, if at all, for married life and relating to a woman. Maybe she did know, but I certainly wasn't listening! I had no qualifications for being married other than I had fallen in love. My first promise of any kind was my vow to Diane in our marriage ceremony. I quickly broke it. Spending much of this marriage deployed overseas and, while I might have been a reliable, trustworthy SEAL, I was far from being a husband with any integrity. In other words, I cheated. I was a royal asshole. I also lacked the communication skills necessary for a successful marriage, although I didn't know this either at the time.

Next, I married a smart and successful advertising wiz named Ellen. Deciding that infidelity was my issue, and that it obviously didn't work to cheat in a marriage, I said to myself, *"I WON'T DO THAT AGAIN!"* I became resolute about being faithful, thinking THIS TIME the marriage would work! I still lacked any facility in communicating my feelings. It was as though I had an anchor tied to my leg and didn't know it. Ellen was less patient and far more expressed than Diane—at least from my perspective! After three years, this marriage sunk.

After Ellen, I gave up on marriage until I met Ginny. I figured if I was faithful, AND I listened more intently to womanly needs, I could make my third marriage work. The problem was I had been trained as a SEAL, not a woman's advocate! I still had no idea, compassion nor understanding of the female perspective. Hindsight, they say, is always 20/20.

---

 *Past lessons are not remedies for future expectations. The future is never what you expect.*

---

Ginny brought three loving children into my life— Sarah, Erin and Christopher. She's a great mother. Acting as both parents while I traveled most of the time, Ginny put on a life jacket and survived the marriage for seventeen years. Looking back, I saw that she had surrounded herself with many good friends, specifically girlfriends, who obviously supported her emotionally. I failed at that job! Among many positive qualities she possessed, Ginny was proficient at the secret called, 'steadfastness.' I still see her expressing her proficiency with this particular secret today as she deals with our children in the face of occasional rebellious teenage adversity. (We'll look at 'steadfastness' later.)

After my third divorce, I had to face many disappointments, including my failures in relating to women. When it came to marriage I was a failure! While I went through my share of feeling bad, at some point I realized that feeling bad altered nothing. Calling myself a failure altered nothing either. These feelings served only to displace my responsibility. So, I took responsibility for the demise of my marriages. Had I been responsible before marrying my wives, I would have communicated with them, up front and VERY CLEARLY, that they were marrying a Navy SEAL, not fun-loving Mike Brady (father of six kids on the successful family TV rerun, *The Brady Bunch*.) At some point within each of my marriages my wives wanted me to change, to be more like the neighbors' husbands—the Mike Bradys of the world. When Mike never showed up, they were left disappointed and frustrated in realizing that they were stuck with JACK. This was when their 'missions' began to try to turn me into Mike, but obviously to no avail. In taking responsibility for my failings (not failures), I was no longer victimized by my circumstances. Being responsible (not as to blame myself, but rather as being the cause of the failings) provided me with a sense of freedom and the ability to start to look at marriage, in general, from different perspectives. I recognized, for example, that marriage is a cultural phenomenon and is dependent, to a large degree, on the specific culture into which one is born. Had I been born elsewhere, who knows, I might have possessed a different set of cultural values about romance, or as one admiral I worked for called it, *"He-ing and she-ing!"* Now feeling free and easy, another thought crept up on me. I had failed a hell of a lot more than three times! Why had I only counted my marriages? I had been in relationships with other women who were just as loving, who had also contributed to my life, and who deserved being honored. I had been guilty of 'mafia counting'—that is, choosing only to remember the relationships I felt 'counted.' I'm unsure as to why I never counted them, other than to probably refrain from looking bad to others. This was unconscious and unexpressed, of course. I also had unwittingly avoided confronting my total failure in relationships with ALL women—even with my sister Jill. Taking a long, hard look, I realized that all the women in my life mattered and deserved to be counted. I had been failing in the world of women all my life.

At this point I committed to bringing closure to my romantic relationships. I contacted the women I could find and apologized for destroying the relationships. I then recreated new relationships with all three ex-wives and several of the women I had hitherto ignored—at least the ones who were willing to forgive me.

I am currently married to my fourth wife, Shari Darling, with whom I have been in relationship with for almost five years. With Shari, I am finally FULLY self-expressed! Lucky for me, Shari is a lot like Jiminy, impervious to my SEAL-like intensity. She's proficient at the SEAL secrets, 'volunteer and tough.' When this lion roars, she remains cool. Sometimes she raises her eyebrows and grins and brings attention to the poetry—the metaphors and similes—in my 'sailorlike' language. Shari finds the humor in it all. Never victimized, she is a volunteer in her own life and certainly in relationship with me. She loves me AND more importantly, she actually likes JACK. On a daily basis she says, at least once, in response to something I've said, *"Jack, that's DISGUSTING!!"* Then she proceeds to fall over laughing. She enjoys my Navy SEAL (aka 14-year-old boy) humor. You could say we are like SEAL swimming buddies . . . with the requisite plumbing differences.

> *No one can make you feel inferior*
> *without your consent.*
>
> -Anna E. Roosevelt

While I could fail in my fourth marriage, I will not declare myself a failure and become a priest. I keep polishing the SEAL secrets and am committed to giving and having romantic love in my life. I experience the extreme good fortune of having lived such a rich or rather colorful life.

You might intend to have one marriage or one relationship in your lifetime. I commend you for this.

But I also ask you this . . . is it really one? Or, have you also been mafia counting? Do you honor and count all your past partners? How many partners have you discounted? If you have had or intend to have one relationship until death do you part, you will want to polish a few of these SEAL secrets, beginning with 'commitment' and 'steadfastness.' And as you will see later on, great marriages are made up of two people both expressing, beyond commitment and steadfastness, another SEAL secret called, 'operator.'

To be extraordinary is to embrace your romantic failings, despite how few or how many you have had. To be extraordinary is to acknowledge and honor ALL partners who have touched your life, whether for one hour, one year, a decade or an entire lifetime.

Our North American culture dictates that failing means something about us. We love sports, and in every game, someone wins and someone loses. We focus on the winners without considering the countless failings that took them to their victory. We understand the principles, but understanding something makes little difference. Countless types of extraordinary people all have something in common—they learned that failing to succeed is part of living extraordinarily. I once read that Thomas Edison made four thousand attempts to invent the electric light bulb. When he finally succeeded, his assistant was carrying that bulb to a demonstration and dropped it!

In BUD/S, one of the volunteers named Al Baldwin could barely swim, and his inability to swim occurred to me as strange. SEALs are known as frogmen because of their superior swimming ability. I was stunned that a guy could be so foolish as to put himself in this particular training without having any ability in this most important skill. During swimming phases (classes), Baldwin looked like a drowning puppy. He received extra attention from the instructors. (Extra attention was NOT a positive or fun thing.) In spite of his incredible lack of prowess, he made it through BUD/S. Baldwin's determination and stick-to-it-ness inspired me. Lectures on positive thinking and a 'rah-rah' attitude were unnecessary for him. He simply did what he said he would do. By the time BUD/S completed, Baldwin was a competent swimmer and a Navy SEAL. We all considered Baldwin to be extraordinary! It was his attitude!

In BUD/S we learned that the future is NEVER what you expect. So, while planning your future and preparing for emergencies may be commendable, watch out that you don't get too emotionally attached to a particular outcome. Deal with the obstacles you encounter moment to moment, keep going despite repeated failings and let your future take care of itself. SEALs are experts at overcoming repeated failings, in every moment, so as to deal with the reality of what is actually happening. If you learn to continually overcome repeated failings, shortening your recovery time to begin anew in that moment, you will have the ability to recreate your life as extraordinary. When you are extraordinary as a matter of routine, the universe will respond positively. When this happens, your future will possess endless and unexpected possibilities. If you find yourself unwilling or unable to let go of your failings, keep in mind that one thousand years from now, no one and not even you, will care or remember.

Imagine what you could accomplish if you allowed yourself to fail over and over again without having it mean something self-defeating. Imagine what your life would be like if you had not given up on your dream to own your own business, be a rock star, hockey player, movie star, doctor, lawyer, financial advisor, mother or author. Here is the good news: you can recreate your life as extraordinary right now. And while you may not be able to fulfill on old dreams, you can create new ones, knowing you now have access to utilizing this secret to help you succeed.

# Evolution for Personal Growth:

Read this chapter again.

**Purpose of Evolution:** To have you deal with your fears around failing.

**Action:** Choose one activity that you have been considering and NOT DOING ANYTHING ABOUT. For example:

- Writing a book.
- Starting your own business.
- Going back to high school or college to get your degree.
- Playing in a band.
- Anything the achievement of which would have you FINALLY be all right with yourself and be able to get YOU to believe you are unbeatable if accomplished! (This does not mean you now have the right to go out and stalk that 'perfect' mate who won't date you. Or, jumping off a building flapping your arms real fast. In other words, be realistic.)

Write a list of your explanations, justifications and good excuses for why you have not undertaken this project to date. Wait forty-eight hours and reread the list. Next, crumple the list and burn it! Get a mentor in this specific area. For example, if you intend to write a book, join a writer's group or sign up for a writing class. If you are obtaining a mentor, be sure to create a list of actions, including dates and times, as to when you will initiate and complete on each step towards thefulfillment of this project. Your mentor is to keep you accountable to your promises.

# Let Us Recap:

You've now gone through evolutions for six secrets in your BUD/S training. If you have read the chapters, implemented the evolutions, you're ready to enter the TEAMS as a novice SEAL.

But before entering the teams, let's look at what you might have discovered through your training, in actually performing your evolutions, about what it takes to possess an unbeatable attitude and to recreate your life as extraordinary . . .

# EXTRAORDINARY PEOPLE:

- Know that their lives are based on free will.
- Live as though their lives are at stake. They accept that life offers no guarantees or security. They are aware of 'reality' instead of indulging their illusions.
- Celebrate who they are, despite their human-ness, and do not try to be like others, and yet are willing to learn from others.
- Are disciplined (highly trainable.)
- Relate to failing as part of the success process.
- Know that most everything is possible.
- Keep their promises and word to others and to themselves as though their lives depend upon it.
- Plan time for the unexpected.
- Apologize when they cannot keep their word, break their promises or are in the wrong without justifications and excuses.

# *Your Insights:*

# PART TWO

## The TEAMS

*You're entering the TEAMS!*
*And . . . you're on probation!*

*Time to start all over again.*
*How do you like them apples, Bunky?*

# INTRODUCTION

# *Starting Again*

# Introduction

## *Starting Again*

When a successful trainee is assigned to a SEAL team, he is often uncertain about his place amongst the experienced SEALs and in the grand scheme of things. While having just completed what is considered the single most arduous training regimen in the U.S. military, he still considers himself a beginner in his new environment. The SEALs who were in the teams prior to his arrival had completed the same training as himself and now have operational experience. What the successful trainee finds, for the most part, is that he is accepted by his more experienced teammates. Yet, there remains for him having to demonstrate to his teammates that the BUD/S instructors made the right choice in graduating him. In very short order, he is either displaying the attributes cultivated at BUD/S or he's kicking back and acting like he's already got it made, e.g., telling stories about his BUD/S training like HE was the first to go through the program!

Inside the 'SEAL culture,' no one gives a rat's ass about the trainee's stories. The SEALs concentrate on the job at hand, not a guy's stories of making it through kindergarten. By the time the trainee is designated as a fully qualified SEAL, his experience is frequently anticlimactic.

For the rest of his SEAL career, however long it is, the trainee is always subject to being de-designated based on his performance or lack thereof, both on or off duty. The trainees have a saying that captures this reality, which is first learned at BUD/S: 'The only easy day was yesterday.'

Are you ready for the TEAMS?

# CHAPTER SEVEN

# The Sixth Secret: Be Committed (Like You've Never Imagined Possible)

# Chapter Seven

## The Sixth Secret: Be Committed

## (Like You've Never Imagined Possible)

*Work consists of whatever a body is obliged
to do . . . play consists of whatever a body is
not obliged to do.*

—Mark Twain
(The Adventures of Tom Sawyer)

To be committed is to be bound emotionally and intellectually and, some might say, spiritually, to an idea, principle, course of action or to someone. It is to pledge, to promise, or vow not only to yourself but also to SOMEONE ELSE. It is to maintain this bond you made of your own free will on a moment-by-moment basis. If you make and/or keep a promise to yourself, this is called being resolute, a sort of 'you against the world' approach. Being resolute is frequently accompanied by the experience of hard work and little joy, and is in the category of New Year's Eve resolutions.

Even when committed, you will still retain your wants, whims, desires, etc. The commitment you create is YOU saying to another person(s) that your commitment supersedes these wants, whims, desires, or feelings, etc. By stating your commitment aloud, you allow others the opportunity to hold you accountable in times when you feel like giving up or when you think the grass is greener. It always is. The joke is . . . when you go to where the grass is greener, you'll be there, too—looking for the greener grass. We call this being a cow. Have you ever heard the saying, 'No wonder the grass is always greener over there . . . cause you're killing the grass under your feet!' *(Well, maybe it's a bad saying.)*

. To be committed is not in wanting something badly. It is not saying, *"I am committed."* It is also not trying REALLY hard, doing your best or merely saying, *"I'll do it."*

---

 *Commitment goes BEYOND every justification to quit.*

---

Commitment is two sided: there is what you will accomplish inside your commitment, and what you WON'T accomplish because of your commitment. This is the nature of commitment, no matter the specific commitment you choose.

I ran into a friend who had been married and divorced a couple of times and had become gun shy. (In this case it was NOT me.) In other words, he resisted having another romantic relationship. Then he met the perfect woman and was beside himself. HE WANTED to marry her. Before they married, he created a pre-nuptial agreement. The agreement essentially allowed him to do anything he wanted to do, sexually and economically. (Hugh Hefner could have learned a thing or two in this deal!) This was my friend's answer to succeeding and fixing what had not worked in the two failed marriages. His fiancé signed the agreement. He told me about this including all the lurid and graphic details. I asked, *"Why the hell are you getting married? Why not stay single?"* He said, *"Because we love each other, Jack!"* Knowing I was incapable of offering him anything useful in this area at this time—his mind was set on his solution—I left it at that. Not long afterwards, the marriage failed. He had essentially remained single inside his commitment to be married. Obviously, he honored his drive to be single (and his other 'drives') above his commitment to be married. He asked for and received everything he wanted . . . and the marriage still failed! This is called outsmarting oneself or as they say in the Navy, 'messing up a wet dream!'

Without commitment, you are at the mercy of your whims, wants, don't wants, desires, feelings, and bright ideas. Only you can determine to what you will be committed. If you are awake and adult, you will realize that consequences exist for any commitment . . . AND YOU NEVER KNOW WHAT THE CONSEQUENCES ARE IN ADVANCE!

---

 *Commitment is ALWAYS stepping into the unknown. The future is never what you expect, so how can you KNOW what your commitment will hold?*

---

If you are competent or masterful at something, saying you are committed to 'it' is phony, because you are already 'it' whatever 'it' is. I don't tell people I'm committed to being a man because I'm already that.

When I discovered at age thirty-four that I was suppressing my love for and from the people I loved, I had what is called, in some circles, an epiphany. When my Uncle Jake died some ten years previously, I experienced my profound sadness for never telling him how much I truly loved him. I was wracked with grief. Having automatically adopted the culture and one of the many customs of the area in which I grew up, I had become quiet, withheld, and unexpressed except in my career. No longer willing to be a miser with my love, I created a commitment to be fully expressed. This commitment was, at first, very uncomfortable. For example, I did not experience a good, warm sensation when I expressed my love to my father. In fact, doing so felt phony and awkward at first. But despite the discomfort, I remained committed to expressing my love and so generated the words, even though I felt nothing at the time. Over time, expressing my love to the people I loved became easier and even pleasurable. This commitment literally altered the course of my life and my relationships. When you get to a place in your relationships where expressing love through your words and actions becomes comfortable, you can actually go beyond this. The expression of your love can become transparent. This is the state of my relationship with my brother Mike. Our mutual love and respect is ALWAYS present, with or without words, with or without actions. It just is. And I'm not talking about the transparency many people experience in relationships— such as taking the other person for granted. I actually experience palpable love while I am in my brother's presence. While my sister Jill and I live far apart and see each other less often, I experience the same depth of love for her, as well.

*Our doubts are traitors,*
*and make us lose the good we oft might win,*
*by fearing to attempt.*

—William Shakespeare
(All's Well That Ends Well, I, IV)

People can make two kinds of commitments—a commitment to benefit oneself and/or a commitment to serve others. While someone can commit to serve oneself, no one ever commits to ONLY serving others. This is a huge fallacy. Selflessness is the attribute of a saint. To think of one's self as selfless is to be the opposite—self-absorbed. Everyone committed to something outside themselves is ALSO committed to themselves. It is a two-sided proposition. Even when serving others, we are serving ourselves, though we might not be aware that we are. For example, we might simply be fulfilling an inner desire to be a good person. This is honorable, but still self-serving. And there is also nothing wrong with this. It is an aspect of being human.

To be unbeatable, however, you might want to consider creating a commitment larger than yourself.

*Existence will thereby become harder for him*
*in every respect than it would be if he lived*
*for himself.*
*But at the same time it will be richer, more*
*beautiful and happier.*
*It will become, instead of mere living, a real*
*experience of life.*

—Albert Schweitzer

When a trainee applies for BUD/S, something motivates him. There are reasons—be it to prove that he can get through the training, to serve his country, to utilize the qualities he thinks he has for the greater good, because it seems like a good idea, or a combination of two or more of these ideas. My assessment is that very few who begin or finish BUD/S do it solely to serve their country. Most young men have but a conceptual grasp of what their country is, such as a set of arbitrary boundaries decided long ago or a series of declarations by our forefathers or some other version learned in a high school civics class. In other words, 'my country' is something passed on from previous generations so much so that it rings with nobility to the inexperienced. When committed to an ideal or principle greater than oneself, a person can do extraordinary things that, if attempted alone, would rarely take place. A person who has difficulty losing weight, for example, and is known for failing at this, might suddenly be inspired when this commitment becomes an effort to support other people in living full, healthy and productive lives. (I suspect this is some form of Richard Simmon's commitment— the diet and exercise guru.)

In entering BUD/S the trainees have personal commitments they intend to fulfill, as well as a collective, greater commitment to serve their country, no matter how fledgling their understanding of this concept may be. They are committed to something greater than their own lives for the common good. If they are in BUD/S solely for selfish reasons, they are usually unsuccessful in completing the rigorous training designed around teams.

So while it is honorable to be committed to making money, traveling the world, losing weight, selling a million CDs, getting that lead role in a movie, owning a yacht, creating a family, what commitment might you create that is greater than yourself—that is if you intend to use your uniqueness and live your life as extraordinary? In other words, what is your life about?

*How do I use my whole life, my whole self to*
*bring some goodness into the world?*

—Oprah Winfrey (Biography, TV Show)

We need only look at the extraordinary people we can remember throughout history to see they were committed to something greater than themselves— Mother Teresa, Mahatma Gandhi, Martin Luther King, George Carlin.*

Look to what you are presently committed. Your actions will tell you. You may want to be in a committed romantic relationship, but what do your actions reveal? Remember the old adage, 'Actions speak louder than words?' It is OLD. The senior version is, 'Your actions are ALWAYS a product of your words, and the words that determine you are mostly obscured from your view.' Be prepared if your loved ones, friends and coworkers confront you about your lack of commitment. They are simply responding to your actions, often contrary to what you might have stated aloud as your commitment.

When actions are disharmonious with a commitment, human beings often experience emotional suffering or resignation or indulge in drugs and alcohol. They numb themselves to reality. When a person is fulfilling a commitment, life is satisfying, joyful, and full of possibilities, despite any hard work that might be involved. On a television episode of *Biography*, Oprah Winfrey was asked if being 'Oprah' was a burden for her to carry. She replied, *"Oprah is dancing in the streets!"*

Ask yourself, *"To what am I committed?"* The idea is not to find the answer but to live from inside of this

---

* *George Carlin, in his own way, makes a difference in the world through language by revealing and pointing out our human absurdities.*

question. Why a question? Questions lead us to inquire and be open to look at our actions versus our words of good intentions. An answer gives us access to only one thing—one answer, or as they say in railroading, narrow gauge rails.

> *The first key to wisdom is constant and*
> *frequent questions . . . for by doubting*
> *we are led to question and*
> *by questioning we arrive at truth.*

—Peter Abelard

When living from inside a question, we see our inconsistencies. We can then take actions that return us to our commitment. This provides choice and free will.

Many people pride themselves on working hard without ever examining what these terms actually imply. I've been amazed at the number of people who, upon learning that I'm a former Navy SEAL, have said, *"Man! That must have been really hard doing that stuff!"* In looking back I can honestly say that hard work never occurred to me. Like Oprah, I was dancing in the swamps. For me it was FUN! I had chosen to be a volunteer. I was fulfilling a boyhood dream. Hard work is frequently work that you think is thrust upon you or work that you have to do, rather than something you've volunteered to do.

---

 *If you think that you are working too hard, consider that you are relating to yourself as a victim, not a volunteer.*

---

People often mistake discomfort for hard work.

Discomfort is the by-product of expanding one's capabilities, such as in increasing one's endurance in sports or acquiring new knowledge in business. Ironically, the more you are uncomfortable, the more alive you are. Seeking comfort, on the other hand, brings you closer to being comfortable and deadened to your own life. Most of us learn that SAYING we are committed and acting as though we are working hard is enough to thrive in life. They are not!

---

 *Commitment gets you into life's game. It is but the foundation of survival. Period.*

---

When the going gets tough, most people act like gerbils on a training wheel. They become resolute and continue to work harder, even without results. They do what THEY do best, going faster and faster, but always in the same direction, heading for the same destination—future failings. So what do people require to thrive beyond commitment? It's called being steadfast in their commitment.

# Evolution for Your Romantic Partnership:

Read this chapter again.

**Purpose of Evolution:** To provide you with the opportunity to experience freedom associated with being fully committed in your partnership or marriage on a moment-by-moment basis. (A marriage ceremony is one small expression of a commitment. Unless honored and developed moment to moment, the marriage can take on all the joy and freedom of two animals in a cage at the zoo. You wouldn't call those animals committed . . . more like 'trapped or confined.' You could even put a ring on both animals' paws . . . they still are not committed.)

**Action:** To experience the freedom associated with being fully committed to another, keep a pad and paper readily available so that you can identify and then document those internal thoughts and feelings and/or the external actions you take that run contrary to your commitment. This might include:

- INDULGING internal conversations or fantasies about you with a different partner. (Everyone has thoughts and fantasies. To INDULGE is to plan or undertake actions that are consistent with your fantasy.)
- Gossiping to your friends and family about your 'bad' partner that has you be the victim and the other, the oppressor (bully) in the relationship. Keep in mind that we don't think ourselves as victims, but rather that the other person REALLY IS a certain way.
- Sulking or being nasty because your partner is

not living up to YOUR expectations. These actions are part of your 'hidden agenda' to get your own way. They are not expressions of commitment.

Notice when these internal conversations or external actions are contrary to your romantic commitment and are leaving YOU upset, frustrated, angry, disheartened, resentful, etc. Your next step is to take full responsibility for your lack of commitment. Your lack of commitment has NOTHING to do with the other person's actions or lack of them. It has to do with you keeping your word, period. Once you understand that you are fully responsible for your commitment, communicate with your romantic partner and share with him/her all the internal conversations and/or external actions that have had you being uncommitted in thought and/or deed. THIS COMMUNICATION WILL BE THE RE-CREATION OF YOUR COMMITMENT TO YOUR PARTNER. IDENTIFYING YOUR LACK OF COMMITMENT, SHARING IT WITH YOUR PARTNER IS AN ONGOING PROCESS THAT BRINGS ABOUT FREEDOM AND JOY IN THE RELATIONSHIP. (Engaging in infidelities regularly as long as you communicate and clean up the mess, are the actions of a sneaky, childish manipulator, not a partner committed to joy and freedom within the relationship.)

*Your Insights:*

# CHAPTER EIGHT

# The Seventh Secret: Be Steadfast (The Heart of Commitment)

# Chapter Eight

## The Seventh Secret: Be Steadfast

## (The Heart of Commitment)

*After a forest fire in Yellowstone National Park, forest rangers began their trek up a mountain to assess the inferno's damage. One ranger found a bird literally petrified in ashes, perched statuesquely on the ground at the base of a tree. Somewhat sickened by the eerie sight, he knocked over the bird with a stick. When he gently struck it, three tiny chicks scurried from under their dead mother's wings. The loving mother, keenly aware of impending disaster, had carried her offspring to the base of the tree and had gathered them under her wings, instinctively knowing that the toxic smoke would rise. She could have flown to safety but had refused to abandon her babies. Then the blaze had arrived and the heat had scorched her small body. The mother had remained steadfast. Because she had been willing to die, those under the cover of her wings would live.*

(This story is based on an article in National Geographic sent to me by my ex-wife, Ellen, by e-mail.)

To be steadfast is the demonstrated ability to stand fast in one's commitment no matter what the world throws at you or what you throw at yourself. Once you have established your commitment, there may be some aspects you haven't considered, such as, can you stand fast in this commitment no matter what? Is it worth your life? What is presently stopping you from expressing this commitment now?

BUD/S challenges the steadfastness of the volunteer's commitment to be a Navy SEAL on a moment-by-moment basis and on several levels. This is done while the trainee is provoked, taunted and challenged by the SEAL instructors. At its most basic form, the instructors are merely talking. Their talking never bothers the trainee when he is doing well. In fact, their talking often seems humorous. When the trainee struggles in an area where he is incompetent, their talking sounds like taunting, tormenting and insulting.

The trainees must overcome internal and external adversity simultaneously. Just like in life! The SEAL instructor's job is to challenge the trainee's steadfastness to his commitment. The trainees who remain committed despite failing after failing develop in themselves the skills and temperament to be Navy SEALs, and then graduate with an attribute called 'steadfastness.'

*Fire is the test of gold; adversity, of strong men.*

—Lucius Seneca
(On Providence, Moral Essays)

One thing will ALWAYS interrupt or break down your commitment—your reasons. To reason is to be logical. Any commitment that is worthwhile will challenge you to be illogical and unreasonable. When the going gets tough, people frequently decide to justify their actions for quitting unless they really understand that their lives and the lives of others are at stake.

People, by nature, expect life to be predictable, safe, guaranteed and most of all, comfortable. Herein lies the challenge in creating a commitment. The moment you commit, in short order, life becomes uncomfortable. At best, temptations arise. You begin to question and possibly consider dishonoring your commitment; at worst you pretend you were uncommitted all along. Commitment is often difficult to maintain, especially when one's inspiration subsides. Commitment has you operate outside of your comfort zone and in areas where you are incompetent.

*Things are always at their best in their beginning.*

—Blaise Pascal, Lettres Provinciales

To be unbeatable means embracing discomfort, but not blindly, such as running despite a broken leg or heart condition. It is to function outside of your feelings that would have you be comfortable and ensure predictability. Feelings are valid, but the one constant about feelings is that they will change moment to moment. One moment you might feel inspired about your commitment; the next moment, you don't and are scared. Or you feel defeated. Anyone who has been married for a substantial period of time knows that there are many times when you don't FEEL like being married. To base one's marriage commitment or one's life on transitory feelings is the same as basing your life on the weather, e.g., going to work on sunny days. To be steadfast is to do so despite the endless reasons and feelings that arise from within.

*When faced with the choice to fulfill or revoke the commitment, your reasons WILL occur as powerful forces of possible action!*

At the beginning of BUD/S we had, what many of us now consider, the greatest lecture ever. A senior instructor (the aforementioned Bernie Waddell) stood at the front of the classroom in the Quonset Hut. This was our training introduction on day one. Instructor Waddell proceeded to tell us the statistical chances of us making it through BUD/S. Peering over the top of his glasses, he looked at all of us—about seventy-seven trainees—and said, *"In six months when this class is finished, there will only be enough of you left to fill up a phone booth. Look to your left and right, men . . . at least two people on each side of you won't be here. Two people on either side of you WON'T be here. Do you understand? There will only be enough left to fill a phone booth."*

He went on to tell us that over the years, he had collected a series of out-processing forms. (This was a form that trainees filled out upon quitting BUD/S.) This form allowed the trainees to explain why they had quit. He went on to repeat that almost no one wrote, *"I just couldn't hack it. I just couldn't do it."* The majority of quitters had 'legitimate' reasons.

Instructor Waddell proceeded to recite the reasons, repeating each one THREE times, and each time more emphatically than the last. Here is the list of reasons that caused committed trainees to ring the bell:

---

### REASONS FOR QUITTING BUD/S

- I can't run.
- I can't run in the sand.

---

- I can't run uphill.
- I can't run in Boon Dockers.
- I don't like running.
- I can't.
- My feet hurt.
- My lungs hurt too much.
- The chafing's killing me.
- I have shin splints.
- I have a headache.
- My mother/wife doesn't know I'm here.
- I miss my family.
- I didn't know it would be like this!
- It wasn't what I expected.
- I can do it, but I must be lazy.
- I punched an instructor.
- I bit a blasting cap in two.
- I broke a leg.
- I twisted an ankle and kept running on it.
- My football knee came back.
- I have too much scar tissue.
- My tennis elbow really hurts.
- I can't do pushups.
- I can't do pull-ups.
- My ass hurts.
- I had a death in the family.
- One leg is longer than the other.
- I don't have any clean skivvies. Honest!
- I have chronic insomnia.
- I got a Dear John letter.
- My wife told me to get out.
- My wife said, "It's either the SEALs or me!"
- My dad said, "It's too dangerous."
- My car broke down.
- I have flat feet.
- I'm too far out of shape.
- I'm lonely.

- I've got to see my girlfriend!
- I got a girl pregnant.
- I just got pissed off.
- I made it all the way, but failed a ten-question quiz and they dropped me.
- I went all the way through Hell Week and then decided that I didn't want to be a frogman/ SEAL.
- I took all their shit and then told them to jam it.
- Those assholes are too crazy.
- Training was easy, but I tore up my arm.
- My body couldn't take the cold.
- My body couldn't take the heat.
- I was allergic to explosives.
- I caught the clap.
- They dropped me during Hell Week because they said I was a wise guy.
- Didn't you hear? They dropped me the last day of training.
- I didn't like it.
- I hurt my back pushing another guy on the run.
- My buddy talked me into quitting.
- Seeing a barracuda got to me.
- Saw one shark too many.
- I had a personality conflict with an instructor.
- They didn't like my attitude when I said, "I'm from Missouri, show me!"
- I 'showed up' an instructor in Judo Class.
- I had the worst case of blisters the doctors ever saw.
- I was going great; the doc made me quit.
- They wouldn't let me go to church.
- Being a black belt Judo instructor . . . I didn't want to hurt anyone.
- I'm getting out of the Navy.
- Personal problems.
- It wasn't meant to be.

- Had the flu.
- Fell off an obstacle and cracked my skull.
- Afraid of heights.
- I have claustrophobia.
- I was tired of being cold, wet and tired.
- I can't stand cold food.
- The instructors picked on me.
- I didn't know it was going to be like this.
- I thought this would help me in my marine biology career (I majored in it in College.)
- The instructors are crazy a-holes!
- You've got to be crazy to do this and I'm not crazy!

In going through BUD/S over the next six months, I experienced most of these reasons first hand. They were powerful, all right! Most of the time I was exhausted, wet, cold and sore. Then I would remember Instructor Waddell's talk and say to myself, *"Okay, so I'm freezing my ass off and I'm GOING TO DIE. Tough shit. This would make a hell of a funeral . . . which I won't have to worry about since I'll already be dead."*

*A man's dying is more the survivor's affair*
*than his own.*

—Thomas Mann
(The Magic Mountain, 1924)

Then I took my head out of the dark place it had been located, such as thinking only about myself, looked around and saw that everyone else was in the same straits. Instead of indulging my reasons, I just identified them as B.S. and kept going. Reasons look mighty appealing when one's discomfort level is seemingly unbearable. In looking back at our reasons to justify quitting, however, they often seem ridiculous. Read the above chart again. You might notice how ridiculous these reason were that caused highly qualified and committed trainees to quit on their life long dream.

What were the reasons you told yourself for quitting on your last commitment or lifelong dream? Chances are, if you were to write down these reasons, you'd see that they are no doubt as ordinary as the ones you see above.

---

 *To be steadfast is in expressing your commitment over time and when life becomes extremely difficult.*

---

We have all experienced being acutely aware in the exact moment that we are challenged to break our commitment and are tempted by that Hot Fudge Sundae, or hot 'something.' It feels as though our world stands still until we choose!

To be steadfast is doing so when it appears as though things are out of your control. Breaking one's promise to be faithful in a committed romantic relationship, for example, is not something that 'just happens' to a person, like an accident. *"Yeah, Bob! I was just walking down the street and her genitals attacked me!"* or *"But Honey, it was the booze. I had no control. It just happened before I knew it."* Or *"I did it because you're never home."* One's commitment is not broken because of something outside one's self, such as having a 'crazy' spouse that is driving you to cheat, or a temptress's seduction, or the circumstances or party favors. Many people consciously and unconsciously (and often conveniently) act victimized to justify breaking their commitment. It is a choice YOU make—in a single moment—to satisfy your feelings above honoring YOUR commitment. When you break your promises, have the guts to call a spade a spade. Besides, the primary person who is diminished by your reasons for breaking your commitment is YOU.

There is a difference between breaking and revoking your commitment. Revoking your commitment is not a bad thing. Sometimes revoking a commitment is appropriate. To be unbeatable, talk straight and revoke your commitment in a way that does not blame, hurt, dishonor or disrespect the other person(s) involved— DESPITE how he/she may have behaved toward you. I'm sure you have heard, *"Yeah, well, I slept with his best friend because he screwed around on me first! I'm giving him a taste of his own medicine."* This is not justifiable behavior; it is simply vengeful. To break your commitment because someone did it first is ordinary and downright childish. Your commitment has NOTHING to do with the actions of others. It is your commitment to keep your word, despite how others act. To REVOKE your commitment with honor is extraordinary. If you disagree with this point of view about revoking one's commitment, then you might well be in reaction to your feelings of hurt, disappointment, sadness and/or even betrayal rather than creating actions, despite your feelings, that are aligned with your commitment. It is your responsibility and your choice alone to revoke a commitment if you choose.

A woman in one of my SEAL workshops once told me she had had a six-month affair with another man because her husband was not fulfilling her 'needs.' She felt her actions were justified. Since she and her husband had agreed that her commitment was initially based on her having her needs met, I told her that she did have every right to revoke the commitment. But she had not revoked her commitment; she had broken it. I asked her to consider that, since she brought up the subject and sounded as though she might be suffering, she no doubt felt troubled by her actions. How did I know this? She was trying to convince me to agree with her that she had done the right thing, given her hopeless situation. The conundrum was that she was the one who appeared to be troubled. I told her that she most likely felt troubled because she had not revoked her commitment with honor and in a respectful way, but instead, had broken her commitment clandestinely, six months prior, and had continued to lie to her husband by withholding this information. She had therefore violated HER own code of honor. My perspective seemed 'true' for her, she said.

---

 *Violating your OWN ideals, principles, morals or code of honor is certain to produce one's own DIS-EASE—in some circles called suffering.*

---

Had the UDT/SEAL instructor staff suddenly announced in the midst of training that we were now shifting our mission to be painters or ballet dancers, I would have revoked my commitment immediately!

On a realistic scale, if you are committed in a relationship based upon mutual respect and honoring the other person, and your partner proceeds to verbally or physically abuse you, this would mean the other person has broken the commitment. Your partner has, through his/her actions, made the commitment null and void without the courage to openly say so. It would be criminal on your part to remain in that relationship. Remaining in that relationship, then, would no longer be based on your commitment, but on some inner reason or hope you might have to justify this action in hopes of the future being different. Being committed, at any cost, is silly. Your commitment is YOUR commitment. You made it, so you can revoke it. It's how you fulfill or revoke your commitment that will have you be extraordinary . . . OR acting like a three-year-old.

To be steadfast must not be confused with resignation or blind stupidity! A person might think, in remaining at a job or in a marriage for thirty years, he/she is being steadfast. This may be true. There are couples that remain as great companions and even loving ones well into their golden years. Many people also remain in their careers because they are committed, enjoy what they do, and year after year are challenged and productive. Others are not expressing and/or being steadfast in their commitment, but rather are resigned to how their lives have turned out and are quietly suffering until it is time for 'The Big Sleep.'

Getting your own way—which includes trying to change others to meet your expectations—is also not an aspect of being steadfast. This is not a commitment, has nothing to do with serving others, nor being committed to something greater than one's self or being extraordinary. Getting one's way all the time falls more into the category of being ordinary—being UNTRAINABLE, SELF SERVING AND SELF—ABSORBED.

# Evolution for Personal Growth:

Read this chapter again.

**Purpose of Evolution:** To have you be steadfast.

**Action:** Look at your most significant failure, such as in your romantic partnership, family or career. What were the reasons, explanations you had to justify this failure?

**Action II**: Look at what you are committed to in your life today, right NOW. Write your commitment down on a piece of paper. Under the heading, 'Commitment,' make a list of all the reasons as to why you THINK you have yet to reach your goals and fulfill your commitment. Here are some examples:

I am committed to increasing my level of sales at work.

Reasons for Not Meeting My Goals:

- Our company product is inferior to that of the competition.
- The economy is on the downslide.
- People just are not buying these days.
- I hate my territory.
- I can't be creative. My boss just wants me to sell and thwarts all my ideas.
- I'm stressed because I'm pushed to produce.
- I'm on a down swing in my sales. They don't appreciate me. I'm only as good to them as my last game. They easily forget that I was the BEST salesperson last year!

Look to see if there are similarities between your

past justifications for failing and your current justifications for falling short in reaching your goals. There will be one or two similarities or maybe more. Your job is to find them. When you do find these similarities, you have found the source of what stops you from being steadfast in your commitment. If you cannot see any similarities, consider that you are resisting the evolution. Ask your best friend to assist you—that is for your friend to be ruthless in uncovering these common denominators. Any place you resist your friend is probably a prime area. It's not the time for a namby-pamby friend. You don't need sympathy; you need STRAIGHT TALK. The idea is to identify, ahead of time, what stops you from being steadfast, so that you can, in the future, see this and move beyond the justifications anyway.

*Your Insights:*

# CHAPTER NINE

# The Eighth Secret:
# Be an Operator
# (Anywhere, Anytime)

# Chapter Nine

## The Eighth Secret: Be an Operator

## (Anywhere, Anytime)

*When I'm not thanked at all, I'm thanked*
*enough;*
*I've done my duty, and I've done no more.*

—Henry Fielding (Tom Thumb The
Great, 1730, Act One, Scene One)

In the civilian world, the term 'operator' can refer to a person who has mastered a con game and so is less than admirable. We've heard people say, *"He's a smooth operator."* This description is not the case with regard to this term as used by Navy SEALs and other NATO Special Forces Units. In fact, it is the exact opposite. To be called an operator is the highest compliment or reputation a Navy SEAL can receive from his shipmates. He cannot dub himself one. He earns this reputation. SEALs want operators on their team and by their sides under all circumstances. An operator rises to the occasion. This reputation can be lost at any time by virtue of one's actions or lack of them. The reason? Mistakes can be as deadly as an enemy's bullet.

In the *American Heritage Dictionary of the English Language*, the word 'operate' means to function effectively, to bring about a desired effect or to control the functioning of a well-oiled machine. This is the essence of the SEAL's use of the term. To be an operator is to have the attitude and attributes to understand all aspects of a system (whether this is a military operation, artillery, a ship, a corporation, organization, a movie, a theatre production or even a family) and to have the skills to ensure this system functions effectively like the aforementioned well-oiled machine.

An operator is a professional and more. A professional has skills and experience in a particular field or job and performs these skills well. An operator has skills in a particular field (a professional) AND has a proficient level of experience in other areas of the system.

---

 *An operator is an EXTRAORDINARY professional.*

---

For example, there are many professional basketball players, and there is Michael Jordan, an extraordinary professional. He's an operator. There are many professional artists, and there are extraordinary professionals, such as Picasso, Da Vinci, Van Gogh, and Dali. Every field produces many professionals and a handful of operators.

In the civilian world, a 'system' might be your household or the company you created or where you work. An operator understands how the whole system (household or company) works and is competent to do what it takes to have that system operating like a well-oiled machine. If you work in a company, corporation or organization, you might consider not only learning your job, but going beyond this to understand the business AND the industry in which you work. That's what an operator would do. In other words, be an operator in your job and learn how the entire system operates. Anyone can be an operator, including mothers and fathers, teachers, nurses, police officers, financial advisors/mutual fund wholesalers, CEOs, presidents, vice presidents, executives, professional athletes, actors, managers, small business owners, etc.

Some people think they are operators because they belong to a particular division, group or organization, such as being on an executive team within an organization, or being a professional athlete, or a Navy SEAL. To be an operator is not the function of the job one has. It is how one performs the job.

Being an operator begins with being professional and being able to do your job proficiently. This means doing your job—PERIOD!

*The minute you get away from*
*fundamentals, the bottom can fall out.*

—Michael Jordan
(I Can't Accept Not Trying)

It is not doing your job IF you agree with the system, approve of your boss's personality, religion or ethics, or if your NEEDS are met. It is also not doing your job as long as you are appreciated on a regular basis. It is doing your job despite the lack of agreement, approval, appreciation and acceptance you do or don't receive.

If you need constant acknowledgment by others to be satisfied and engaged in your job, you are not a professional, let alone an extraordinary one (an operator). Rather you are an emotional drain on your team. It means that your relationship to your own word and your level of commitment to your job or marriage is based on external forces, such as the level of emotional support you receive from your boss, clients or romantic partner. Therefore, the level of commitment you have to your own word is about as meaningful as a snail's stool sample. Your ability to produce results in your job is based on the PERSONAL relationship you have with your own word. (You produce results because YOU said so!) This relationship can be created or strengthened with practice. If you offer 'more drama than Shakespeare' and overstate your issues and NEED to be appreciated, you are a squeaky wheel. Operators, while they might be noticed, have no commitment to being the center of attention. They are NOT squeaky wheels. They pride themselves in being the well-oiled wheel.) The paradox, however, is that when one is an operator in the game, he/she stands out as extraordinary to others and often becomes the center of attention. But an operator is not committed nor interested in this. Operators are committed to doing the job on an extraordinary level. While acknowledgement is flattering and often the byproduct of healthy relationships, operators don't NEED, REQUIRE OR DEMAND it. They achieve satisfaction by fulfilling on what they said they would do for others AND for themselves. SEALs, specifically, do not need, require or demand acknowledgement from others. In fact, they often accomplish difficult missions without backup, support or acknowledgement from forces outside their immediate team. Operators take pride in doing their jobs well, period. If you start doing your job at work or in your romantic relationship, chances are you will receive plenty of appreciation whether you need it or not. As the old adage goes, 'The more you give, the more you get!' If I were to properly acknowledge everyone in the SEALs who made a difference in my life, from all the men in my first BUD/S class to my first UDT platoon to my commanding officers, this book would consist solely of listing their names followed by a simple *"Thank You!"*

An operator does exactly what was agreed upon or is expected of him. This is simplistic, and yet the reason many people lose their jobs. They sell themselves, get the job, commit to fulfilling the job description, and then do their own thing, reasoning that somewhere along the line they are fulfilling what is expected despite their lack of results. An operator produces results consistent with the organizational mission, not one's creative expression.

During Vietnam, we had Navy-enlisted men (what might be referred to as low rated/ranked or middle-rated SEALs) who were mercenaries in everything but name. These men lead 50-to 150-man units of former Viet Cong for the purpose of capturing current Viet Cong leaders. Despite their relatively junior status, they were operators and so expressed leadership. They were literally in command, disciplining and leading into combat, these units comprised of ex-VC. Because they had developed themselves as operators through BUD/S and previous combat experience, they operated at a higher level of effectiveness than almost any other similarly rated enlisted men in the Armed Forces. More significantly, their operations were considered the most effective in the Vietnam War.

Operators go beyond what is expected and this begins with paying attention to details. If busy and unable to do a task, an operator knows enough about that task to properly manage the people attending to the details. Paying attention to details means handling the visible and the invisible aspects of a system. This includes looking at all the details—even the most challenging ones or the ones people rarely check. Paying attention to details forces one's attention to the physical world instead of the illusionary world of one's inner dialogue.

*Paying attention to details drives a human being to sanity.*

For example, making money in the restaurant business is a mastered skill or maybe even an art form. The old timers will tell you that there is more to winning in this game than providing customers with great food, great prices, and great service. These are the obvious elements to survive in the restaurant business. Novices often focus on the big picture—that is, finding new and creative ways to increase customer flow and generate a greater profit. BUT—any true master or operator knows—'perfection exists in the details.' The long-term, successful restaurant operators know that making money is largely dependent upon creating a balance between increasing profits and paying attention to and refining the details associated with REDUCING costs.

Paying attention to detail also includes powerful listening. It means to avoid listening to one's own assumptions. We are all experts in listening to ourselves. An operator is awake and so sees and listens to what is taking place in his immediate world and is also constantly aware of what might be needed in the next moment.

If you are hiring someone for a particular job, consider hiring an operator, rather than someone who merely looks good, is charismatic or has lots of glorious ideas. If hiring a general contractor to renovate your home, you might make sure this person is an operator, personally capable of doing the plumbing, electricity and carpentry work himself. You need only ask his past clients to find out if he is an operator or not. This ensures that even if these jobs are sub-contracted, the general contractor will be on the job at all times and have the 'eyes' to see the visible and invisible details to ensure that they are successfully handled. And if the contractor cannot be on the job full time, he checks the details later on to ensure that the sub-contractors handled their work effectively. Sound obvious? (You'd be surprised, as was I, by the number of contractors who do not know how to build a house, and so rely upon the knowledge and expertise of sub-contractors to get the job done.)

The secret 'discipline' is also an aspect of operator. I suggest you read chapter 6 again . . . and again . . . and again. And as you do so, remember . . . I won't make an extra dime!

Operators are also dependable. Dependability means others can trust you. This attribute—trustworthiness—is the greatest gift you can give other people.

We all want operators in our lives. Wouldn't you want someone like Michael Jordan on your team? Well, you're it, Bunky!

When someone is not an operator, you often hear others making excuses and/or defending this person, saying things like, *"I know he is having trouble, but he is such a nice guy."* The biggest excuse/mitigating comment I have ever heard for lack of performance was, *"But, he's a nice guy."* I led seminars in prisons and—I'm actually not being facetious, as newspaper columnist, Dave Barry, might say—the prison inmates were some of the nicest people you could ever wish to meet!

As an example, in my local newspaper I read that Rex Mays, age 42, was convicted of killing Kynara Carreiro, age 7, and her friend, Kristin Wiley, age 10, at the Wiley home next door to his house . . . Mays, who occasionally earned money performing as Uh-Oh the Clown and dressed as Santa Claus and the Easter Bunny, killed the girls the same day he was fired from a low-level warehouse job."

> *And as for being a nice guy I figure sixty to seventy per cent of all the killers that end up in the gas chamber or the hot seat or on the end of a rope are people the neighbors thought were just as harmless as Fuller Brush salesman . . .*

—Raymond Chandler
(The Long Goodbye)

And Raymond underestimated his percentages! So much for the nice guys! Are prisoners and cons dependable? Trustworthy? Hell, NO! They're still screwing around with society's rules and trying to prove how tough they think they are. (Tough is a SEAL secret, one that prisoners lack.) Why do you think they are called cons? Short for convict? Little do they know that they have pulled the greatest con job on themselves! Prisons are society's way of saying, *"You naughty little boy! Go to your room! I'll tell you when you can eat, and when you can go outside to play."* Then you and I pay their babysitters!

I'm not suggesting that all nice guys are killers. I am suggesting, however, that being a nice guy serves to accomplish one thing . . . to have people like you. That might be the game you are up to in life and that is fine. Just remember, however, that being a nice guy is not a secret to have you operating as powerful in the game of being extraordinary. In the SEALs, being a nice guy was a given, like having skin and perfect eyesight. What was required, due to the level of adversity we faced, were EXTRAORDINARY professionals that went beyond merely being professional, reliable or talented. Its name is OPERATOR! As I said earlier, being yourself, being unique gets you into life's game. Being an operator has you THRIVE in the game.

An operator functions as though their job impacts and matters to others; as though everything they do is critical to the mission. No part of the job is beneath them, despite their feelings—like swimming in freezing water at night, and watching human turds float by from moored ships dumping bilges. (You need not wonder why we were there!) Taking pride in one's job, no matter how beneath you or dirty or what that job might entail, is the full expression of an operator. An operator goes beyond the call of duty and handles all the details with integrity.

Operators also make sure they have the ability to do other people's jobs in the event of emergencies . . . which there ALWAYS are! Here are examples of what an 'operator' is NOT:

- Defending your rice bowl, i.e., only doing what you are good at or what the system's rules limit you to do.
- Looking for hobbies or pastimes to take the place of your commitment.
- Doing the minimum to get by.
- Assigning tasks to people who work for you without any interest in what they are doing . . . such as movie and rock stars who are uninterested in management, finances and accounting, and so hire an accountant to do it

> for them! In the Navy this is called 'bending over in the shower!' Hummmmmmm, Babeeee! (This may be my only reference approaching 'salty sailor talk.')
> - Looking for tasks that are important or career enhancing, rather than turning the job you have into one everyone else wants because your performance made it a critical position.
> - Being too busy to do your job.
> - Working eighteen-hour days so as to convince yourself that you are busy.

To get the impact of this secret, take a moment and look at your past failings—in a relationship, job or business. What was missing? Why did you fail? Chances are, if you are honest with yourself and look closely, you will see that you were missing all or some aspects of being an operator. (For example, only doing YOUR job, needing too much attention/acknowledgement, avoiding the idea of mastering details, etc.) Or, you might need polishing in the other secrets. Remember, we all have these attributes, but at various levels. No doubt, if you failed at something, you were operating more by your feelings, wants and desires rather than being committed, steadfast and an operator.

Successful, long-term marriages or life partnerships can be attributed to one or both partners being operators. When the lust is dust, what is left are two people operating within one system, a household. Often, if one partner NEEDS too much attention and the other is not providing it, this need might be fulfilled outside the marriage. This is the act of a child, not an adult and certainly not an operator. If one partner mismanages the finances and/or spends more than the agreed upon budget, or a partner lets the home degenerate into a pigsty, you can be sure that these issues are the basis of major arguments and sometimes separation and/or divorce.

---

*If you have any addictions—alcohol, drugs, sex, shopping, gambling, etc.—you lack complete proficiency within this secret. Addictions keep you from expressing the true YOU.*

---

Everyone wants to be in relationship—romantically and otherwise—with an operator! If you are thinking, *"I'm an operator and my wife isn't,"* don't listen to yourself. Ask your partner! It is a reputation bestowed upon you by someone else.

So to be an operator is the FULL expression of commitment. Because if you choose to do all the things it takes to be an operator, or to be extraordinary, or to ultimately be unbeatable, you will have the capabilities as well as the steadfastness to fulfill your commitments.

# Evolution for Romantic Partnership:

Read this chapter again.

**Purpose of Evolution:** To have you be an operator in your romantic relationship.
**Action:** Pick one activity that your partner has been requesting/nagging you about, such as:

- Cleaning the house.
- Participating in caring for the children.
- Maintenance of the yard, etc.
- Having a romantic evening over and above special occasions.
- Remember to be appreciative without your partner having to ask for it.
- Going out to dinner without having to break the world record for time spent in travel to and from the restaurant. In other words, spending a romantic evening out for dinner that lasts longer than one hour.

Once you've chosen an activity, inform your partner about your new commitment. Create the activity so as to become a 'master' at it, rather than a whining, sniveling crybaby. Once you've mastered the activity, be an operator. This means going OVER AND ABOVE what your partner requests, desires or expects. If you need inspiration, remember . . . you're doing this as an expression of your love for your partner, not because you 'have to.'

## *Your Insights:*

---

## Evolution for Family:

Read this chapter again.

**Purpose of Evolution:** To have you be an operator in your family.

**Action:** Organize a meeting with your family. Allow your partner and children to request and/or decide what they would like to do as an activity in which the entire family can engage. Your job as an operator is to LISTEN! When the family is aligned, it is your job to make it happen. Tell your family that in each month they can decide on a family activity. Don't be surprised that the family aligns on something that you DETEST doing. As an operator, your job is to do the activity anyway, and take pride in doing the job well.

---

*Your Insights:*

## Evolution for Career:

Read this chapter again.

**Purpose of Evolution:** To have you be an operator in your career.

**Action:** Ask your immediate superior (boss) what job/task needs doing that everyone else is avoiding. Take the task on yourself and do it. And don't look for appreciation, a thank you, a promotion or extra pay. Think of this task as something you are doing for your company. If you already know what task needs to be handled, do it. You need not tell your boss that you are doing it. And again, don't look to be appreciated or thanked afterwards.

The more detestable the task, the greater the contribution, and the closer you become to being an operator.

*Your Insights:*

# CHAPTER TEN

# *The Ninth Secret: Be a Teammate (Success is Always a Team Event)*

# Chapter Ten

## The Ninth Secret: Be a Teammate
## (Success is Always a Team Event)

### Do We Have As Much Sense As a Goose?

*Next fall, when you see geese heading South*
*for the winter, flying along in a 'V'*
*formation, you might consider what science*
*has discovered as to why they fly that way.*

*As each bird flaps its wings, it creates uplift*
*for the bird immediately following. By flying*
*in a 'V' formation, the whole flock adds at*
*least 71 percent greater flying range than if*
*each bird flew on its own.*

*People who share a common direction and*
*sense of community can get where they are*
*going quicker and easier because they are*
*traveling on the thrust of one another.*

*When a goose falls out of formation, it*
*suddenly feels the drag and resistance of*

*trying to go it alone, and quickly gets back
into formation to take advantage of the lifting
power of the bird immediately in front.*

*If we have as much sense as a goose, we will
stay in formation with those who are headed
in the same way we are going.*

*When the lead goose gets tired, it rotates back
in the formation and another goose flies point.*

*It pays to take turns doing hard jobs—with
people or with geese flying south.*

*The geese honk from behind to encourage
those up front to keep up their speed. What
do we say when we honk from behind?*

*Finally, when a goose gets sick, or is
wounded by gun shot and falls out of
formation, two geese fall out with that goose
and follow it down to lend help and
protection. They stay with the fallen goose
until it is able to fly, or until it dies; only then
do they launch out on their own, or with
another formation to catch up with their
group.*

*If we have the sense of a goose, we will stand
by each other like that.*

-Source Unknown

Even with a clear understanding of the secrets, it
will take more than you doing it alone to recreate your

life as extraordinary. To be unbeatable is to accept that . . .

---

*Success is a team event.*

---

A team is a group of people with a defined goal or objective. Being a 'part' of a team is one thing; being a worthy teammate is quite another. What is the true essence of a teammate? A teammate, at the level of Navy SEAL, is someone who watches out for his/her teammates, day in and day out, as though his/her life depends upon it . . . BECAUSE IT DOES! It is not someone who looks for ways to manipulate or take advantage of his/her teammates. Being a worthy teammate begins with one being an operator. As we know, operators don't need to be center of attention, and so have no interest in outdoing their teammates.

This is where the secrets and your level of proficiency with them overlap and reveal themselves. When you're on a team, your teammates look at you as though you're a bug being inspected through a magnifying glass. Teammates are the first to see your human-ness (darkness) and your being (light.) A worthy teammate is someone who instinctively knows this and so performs appropriately, effectively and efficiently. A poor teammate is someone who is delusional in thinking he/she might be fooling the other teammates and/or getting away with something. An example of a poor teammate is someone who thinks he's smarter or better, in some way, than the others or believes he/she is the slickest dude on the team. There's no better way to discover the essence or core of a person than to be his/her teammate.

Slick dudes are everywhere, even in the SEALs. They can be charismatic, entertaining, charming and at times, courageous. A common term for slick dudes is B.S. artists. They are the kind of people who would have you believe that they invented ice cream and gave the Wright brothers the schematic for their first airplane. In Vietnam when we were working deep within enemy territory, a slick dude was, at best, worthless, and at worst, a detriment. We didn't need entertainers; we needed operators on our team.

If you are interested in relating to your teammates as though your life depends upon it, you will want to master your proficiency with the secrets. While it is easy to see that your life is at stake in situations that appear life threatening, it is more difficult to really get this on an everyday basis. Until you discover that your life is lived moment to moment and, consequently, every moment wasted is throwing away your life, it is impossible to bring to yourself the recognition of what is required. It is within team that being a volunteer, being disciplined (trainable), being committed, being steadfast and being an operator are needed most.

Who is on your team? Beyond the recreational hockey, baseball or bowling team or your work-related team, you might want to consider that you are actually a member of more than one or two. If you are doing your independent Rambo routine and not consciously relating to your team(s) as necessary for what you are attempting to accomplish, you will end up having a life of puny accomplishments hardly worth mentioning. Teammates are not necessarily in physical proximity to each other, work together or share a house, or like the same hobbies or music. Teammates are people who choose to share a common commitment.

For example, have you ever thought of your family as a possible team? We often think of ourselves as members rather than as teammates of our family. The problem is, as a family 'member' we do not choose our family. As the old adage states, 'We can choose our friends, but we can't choose our family.' Who said so? Choosing includes the ideas of 'wanting' and 'desiring.' If you feel stuck with family members rather than powerfully choosing them (as a place to stand and relate to them), you become a victim rather than a volunteer in your own family. Victims are self-absorbed and only think of themselves. Volunteers, on the other hand, take care of themselves and all family members.

A team is a collection of people coming together to express a common mission and/or to pursue common goals. There is no necessity to form a team within your family if you have no mission, goals or purpose. Family goals can range from creating a celebration to acknowledging someone within the family, supporting a child to attend college, taking a dream vacation together, having a baby or collectively working together to look after an ill family member. A family goal can be as simple as being committed to having harmony and peace amongst all family teammates.

So, if you plan on turning your family into a team of operators, make sure their participation is voluntary. If you attempt to force or manipulate family members into being teammates, chances are you'll end up mollycoddling (babysitting) them and lose sight of your original goals.

If you are resisting the idea of creating team within your family, you might want to look at why. Do you have resentments—hidden or otherwise—toward certain family members? As stated, we often unwittingly view ourselves as victims of our parent(s), siblings or children based on past events or long-ago incidents. We don't think of ourselves as victims, for the most part. We may actually see ourselves as the hero or black sheep in the family and in our recollections of the past. We believe that we did the BEST we could do, given the situations and circumstances we unwittingly found ourselves facing. So, when we share our recollections or memories with others, we leave them with the impression that we were either the hero or the underdog overcoming insurmountable odds over our dysfunctional family member(s).

Being the victim or the hero is not a useful or satisfying position if you are committed to having your family be made up of extraordinary individuals and/or as a team. Remember, to be extraordinary is to recreate in the moment, not allowing previous failings with your family to affect your life RIGHT NOW. Letting go of your position in your family dispute can be downright difficult and may seem impossible. You may think that if you let go of your position and forgive the other member, you are in essence, saying the other member was right, which automatically makes you wrong. That idea is too much for most people to accept. Letting go is to recognize that your position is simply a position . . . rather than THE TRUTH. It is to give up your own arrogance and righteousness. Consider that your REALITY is only the truth for you—even if you have been clever enough to convince yourself and others to buy into your position. More importantly, this reality leaves no room for others to be human and make mistakes. And worse, it leaves little room for you to accept your own mistakes, your own human-ness and to be humble enough to apologize when you have hurt others intentionally or unintentionally. When we hold on to grudges we have NO peace of mind. To recreate your life as extraordinary is to let go of past grudges and give up the notion that others have victimized you. It is to look at your own thoughts and actions and the consequences they create. Remember, forgiving others does NOT absolve them from confronting their own misdeeds. They are responsible to do their own inner work. Forgiving others allows you to have peace of mind.

You may let go of your grudges or position with family member(s), and find, a day or two later, you are back where you started—angry and upset and thinking yourself the hero or underdog again. Letting go takes a ENORMOUS AMOUNT OF FORGIVENESS, COURAGE AND PRACTICE. It does not come quickly or easily. It is a moment-by-moment choice you make. Every time you hear that nasty internal dialogue in your head saying vengeful and righteous comments toward or about your family member(s), you can let it go and recreate your relationship with them in that moment. It is a moment-by-moment choice you will have to make for the rest of your life. So, be patient. Or embrace your impatience.

At age thirty-seven, an event occurred which altered my life. On the evening before my third wedding, Ginny and I went out to dinner with our families to celebrate. Following this marvelous celebratory event, we were headed for our cars when my father turned to me and said, *"Drive slowly, Jack."* I suddenly blew up, telling him to "@*&?~#!%) himself and the horse he rode in on!" Needless to say, I felt seething hostility! As we drove off, my bride-to-be said, *"You were a little harsh with your father back there."* I turned to face her, eyes glared, and I did a verbal Jose Greco (Flamenco dance) on her too! I couldn't believe she had taken his side, and now SHE WAS ALSO CRITICIZING ME! All my life my father had been criticizing me, even on my pre-wedding night!

Three weeks later, as I was sitting at home watching TV, this incident came to mind. I felt profound sadness, knowing I HAD totally overreacted. Then I realized that I had always overreacted this way towards my father for most of my life when I had PERCEIVED him to be criticizing me. For a moment I felt childish. Then I saw that my father's criticism was merely my perception that I unwittingly developed at a young age. All my father had actually said were three words: *"Drive slowly, Jack."* I had reacted as though he had stuck a cattle prod up my nose! While criticism is certainly agreed upon by most people to be a real phenomenon in North America, I believe it is a childish perception, not THE TRUTH! Looking from my father's perspective, I saw that all he wanted was for me to be safe. Why? I drove a Corvette. It took me five seconds to get to a phone and ten minutes to compose myself sufficiently to communicate with him my discovery . . . and to apologize for years of my acting like a nasty brat! Being the loving and compassionate father that he was, he simply replied, *"I knew that, Jack. Don't worry about it."* Funny thing, I never heard my father criticize me again, and he didn't change a bit!

Had I not had this insight and given up my victimized position, I still might, to this day, be dwelling in the idea of how my father had criticized me much of my life. To this degree, I would have robbed myself of the experience of accepting my father's love and of fully expressing my love for him while he was alive.

Your family team can extend beyond the immediate family. If, for example, your husband or wife has an ex-spouse, either 'ex' can be a part of your family team. Sound absurd? To create this, you might have to get outside of your resentments about this ex that has you be 'right' about how WRONG this ex REALLY IS! Here is the paradox: This ex-spouse is part of your extended family whether you like it or not, especially when children are involved! It is merely a matter of how you relate to your extended family and what you have created as a commitment for your life with regard to family that counts.

Keep in mind that while you might get to a place where you consider a family member or this ex as your teammate, he/she does not have to think of you as one. It is best to avoid this expectation. This exercise is about you recreating your life as extraordinary, and you creating YOUR team(s). Feeling uncomfortable with all of this? Good! To be unbeatable involves taking on missions that are seemingly impossible and often uncomfortable, but will have you be extraordinary.

Why not communicate with your family, and let them know that you think of them as one of your teams? Let them know what they mean to you. Tell each teammate what you rely on him/her for and what each teammate can count on from you. The conversations that ensue can create unity and produce goals and objectives for your family team to undertake that you never thought possible. This can be a more rewarding experience than the same old dynamic of obligatory phone calls and visits and pretending to be okay despite hidden resentments. You might just experience feeling loved and alive while in your family's presence, instead of feeling like you are a member of the walking dead. And remember . . .

---

 *Being a teammate is a voluntary occasion.*

---

If you tell your siblings, parents or children that they HAVE to be on your team, it may just backfire. Every person has the option of choosing or declining your request. Remember . . . you want VOLUNTEERS ONLY! Otherwise, you'll have a bunch of victims and a bunch of new problems.

# Evolution for Family:

Read this chapter again.

**Purpose of Evolution:** Creating your family as a team.

**Action:** Call a family meeting. Be sure to have a pad and pen handy. Create a conversation in which you ask your family to think about the idea of them being a team. The idea is for your spouse or partner and the children to view themselves as teammates rather than merely members of a family. It is your job to communicate effectively to your family the benefits of them participating as a team. For example the benefits might be:

- Anyone who has been playing the martyr/Lone Ranger and saying things, such as, *"I do everything around here,"* will no longer live in this fantasy.
- The entire family can contribute towards the children getting good grades at school, including the children themselves. (Having the kids relate to themselves as team players toward this goal is far more effective than them thinking their parents are 'bugging them.' They may also understand that when they don't do their homework, the other teammates worry about them.
- As teammates, your partner and/or children may feel more comfortable to communicate what is bothering them and what they EXPECT from you. (As a parent, you might find out that one of your personal destructive habits is negatively impacting the morale and performance of your other teammates.)

It is your job, since you are the one generating the

team, to create an environment that is SAFE for all teammates to communicate their feelings, needs, dreams, visions and desires. (Be prepared, you may not like what you are going to hear. You may have to promise that there will be no punishment or remonstrations if your teammates tell you their 'truth.') The idea is for each teammate to explain to the others what he/she can be counted on to provide to the team, as well as any expectations he/she might have from the other teammates. Be sure to POST the teammates' promises (what they are delivering for the team.) You can always hold future meetings, much like a football huddle, to restate each teammate's promises, etc.

*Your Insights:*

# The Ninth Secret Continued

## Be a Teammate

## (The Dirty Underwear Nobody Talks About—

## Conflict Works)

 *Team is often an indelicate proposition.*

Many people have expectations that a team should be harmonious and that everyone should get along. (This is a lot of 'should-ing' on oneself.) People also expect, when confrontation arises, that their teammates hold their tempers and communicate in an acceptable tone— a tone that offers a level of comfort . . . perhaps accompanied by a bit of aromatherapy! When conflict arises, many people fight against or resist confrontation, and experience anxiety, grief or victimization. These reactions have them withdraw their full participation. When you are faced with confrontation, how do you react? Walk away? Hang up the phone? Go silent? Get violent? Remain suppressed? Act civil all the while covering up your hidden hostility? Do you gossip to others about the person by whom you are confronted?

All of these reactions arise when people resist conflict. As you might recall, to be committed is to be bound emotionally and intellectually and, some might say, spiritually, to an idea, principle, course of action or to someone. When a married couple, or any group of people (family or coworkers), is bound together in this way with the same common goal, conflict frequently arises. Realistically, what else can you expect, with as many points of view as there are people on the team? It is the meshing together of ideas and principles that produces conflict. Conflict has the potential to produce extraordinary results—if you allow for it. American screenwriter, director, producer and host, Michael Moore, is an example of someone who uses conflict and confrontation to bring awareness to a wide variety of injustices and issues in America. While his most recent documentary film has stirred up a great deal of controversy, 'Bowling For Columbine' has served as an effective means of bringing attention to the problems arising from America's gun culture. Conflict is the juice of life, the key ingredient—not just in Michael Moore's films, but in every play and movie!

Conflict arises when people talk straight. Many people believe that teammates should avoid conflict. The problem is in an attempt to avoid interactions, confrontations and conflict, people instead gossip to others, even the media, who might agree with their point of view, but who CANNOT make a difference or move the team forward. Or, to avoid confrontation, they suppress the issues at hand, sometimes for years.

In combat, Navy SEALs deal with issues and problems directly with the person(s) involved AND in the moment they occur. And because their lives depend upon it, the communications can be bold and assertive!

Bullets move faster than seconds! There is little time for niceties or for a steering committee report or a family council meeting.

Allowing conflict to exist does not mean encouraging or promoting it, or accepting any form of abuse and/or justifying your actions of delivering abuse. This is a different dynamic and reveals a lack of respect for one's self and for others. It also does not mean you have a license to scream and holler at people, in front of the kids or at work! To be extraordinary is to respect ALL your teammates and operate beyond your feelings, not be at the mercy of them. Abuse is an expression of the abuser's feelings of frustration, anger and rage. Abusers are reactive. This is not one being a Navy SEAL or a professional of any sort.

To allow conflict to exist simply means that you act with compassion and understand that the person(s) involved are expressing their feelings and perceptions about the issue at hand. It means you are detached enough to realize and accept that they have every right to their feelings and perceptions, whether you agree with them or not. Did you know that you can respect and honor another's point of view as your own and listen intently and compassionately, whether you agree or disagree? ANY team made up of highly committed people intent on achieving the same goal and producing results will repeatedly face indelicate moments. Indelicate moments are often referred to as a 'falling out,' such as falling out of relatedness. You might instead think of indelicate moments to be a 'falling in' to relatedness. Or think of them as heart-to-heart conversations. It is in the face of conflict that we are given the opportunity to grow emotionally, to see ourselves in the way that our teammates and the world see us, like that bug underneath a magnifying glass. But only if we so choose.

Realizing and accepting that team is an indelicate proposition can produce an opposite effect—it can take the anxiety out of the conflict for you when it arises. The Beatles said it best: *"Let it be."* In other words, you might stop resisting conflict and simply allow it to take place. When you give people the right to their points of view and perceptions, and honor these points of view as you do your own, people feel heard and respected. Their upset, most likely, will disappear. If you are a committed teammate, conflict will arise on your team whether you like it or not. You might view conflict as an aspect of passion that forwards, rather than thwarts, the team's intention and helps in producing results. The key is to stay focused on your team's commitment, not use conflict as a justification or reason to quit!

Often when tragedy strikes a family, conflict arises. We often hear about how the death, abduction, abuse, assault or victimization of a child causes the parents to divorce. It is tremendously difficult for a family team, made up of individuals with their own perspectives, to move through this kind of conflict.

On a personal note, for example, tragedy struck my family with respect to one of my children. Ginny and I came into direct conflict with respect to how the situation ought to be handled. The conflict magnified ALL the grievances that caused the divorce in the first place, ten years earlier. Feelings such as hate, anger, frustration, sadness and grief (all parts of life) existed for me and other family members for an extended period. Like all families, we rode the emotional roller coaster attempting to work through our differences. Having my created our family as team (for me), I was committed, beyond our different perspectives, that the family be peaceful. As is frequently the case, there was no 'right' way to handle or resolve the situation. BOTH our perspectives were valid, as well as those of our present partners, and of course our child, to work through this challenge. Compassion and forgiveness became my personal goal rather than my continuing to experience anger toward family members and hatred and revenge toward the perpetrators. As I stated earlier, experiencing these qualities does not come quickly or easily. On a frequent basis, I still find myself experiencing the emotions of grief, white-hot rage and fantasies of blood thirsty revenge toward the perpetrators—my human-ness. In the moral code in which I was conditioned/absorbed, these perpetrators 'deserved' to die, much more so than any VC I ever fought against and/or killed. After my retirement from the Navy in 1982, I vowed never to kill another human being for ANY reason. (After this family tragedy, remaining true to this commitment has been difficult to maintain.) When I notice that I am experiencing an episode of rage, I let go of it and refocus on my commitment to be peaceful. But these emotions come back again. And when they do, I let go of them again and again. It is a moment-by-moment process that I will no doubt continue for the rest of my life. The point is that our family team's commitment pulled us through our differences, when in fact, any one of us could have 'quit' a dozen times throughout the situation.

How do you deal with conflict? Many people pride themselves on the ability to hold onto grudges. They consider this to be an aspect of strength. I know people who have held on to grudges for a decade, including me! The longer you hold a grudge, the more you are being controlled by your own perceptions and feelings, and the more you are attempting to control others. This is the recipe of suffering. The only person you are truly affecting is yourself. Holding on to resentments and grudges causes 'dis-ease.' A friend of mine once told me that resentment is a poison you swallow and then wait for the other person to die! It is to live as though you are right and everyone else is wrong. This is a grand and glorious illusion and, surprising as it may be, rather ordinary. To be extraordinary is to deal with conflict as it arises, forgive others even without their apology, handle the team's details with precision and to the best of your ability, and stay committed and steadfast to the team.

## Evolution for Your Romantic Partnership:

Read this chapter again.

**Purpose of Evolution:** Creating your romantic partnership as team and learning to deal with conflict.

**Action:** Call a meeting with your partner. Declare a truce. Create a conversation so that your partner understands that you want to create TEAM within the relationship. Be sure to let your partner know that, in this meeting, he/she can say anything without reprisals/recriminations. If your partner disagrees with this idea, tell him/her that the meeting's intention is to re-establish the relationship. It's your job to communicate first. Tell your partner what YOU have been doing or not doing that has disempowered the relationship. Don't be surprised if your partner already knows, acts smug, blurts out comments, such as, *"I'VE BEEN TRYING TO TELL YOU THAT,"* or, *"I'VE TOLD YOU THAT A HUNDRED TIMES."* Or, *"No, S*&T, Dick Tracy!"* Apologize for what you have or have not done. Share your promises for the future with your partner.

*Your Insights:*

# The Ninth Secret Continued

Be a Teammate

(Giving Up the Asinine Arrogance

That Your Opinion Came Down From

a Sacred Mountain on a Stone Tablet)

Communication is an integral part of team. Relating to communication like your life depends upon it makes for an extraordinary team. This means your communication is intentional and purposeful, forwarding the team's common goals. And while a SEAL team's communication is purposeful, it is often insignificant. Any team made up of operators can forward any goal or conduct any mission like a well-oiled machine. Working at an extraordinary level of proficiency often creates, among teammates, a sense of freedom and lightheartedness. When a system is functioning like a well-oiled machine, there is plenty of room for humor and laughter: all the while the teammates remain intentional.

Being responsible for your conversations starts with

you giving up the notion that your opinion came down from a sacred mountain on a stone tablet.

---

 *Being responsible means separating the 'facts' from your 'perceptions.'*

---

(In medical terms, this means performing one's own cranial/rectal extraction.) People often act like their opinion about something is the TRUTH. Or, they manipulate the meaning of words to control situations and other people and to be right about their point of view. A fact is something known to be true. It is what happened. A person might witness what happened, but the moment 'what happened' is turned into words and told to one's self or shared with another, this incident becomes one's biased perception of what happened— an opinion. To perceive something is to obtain knowledge through our senses, to observe, to understand something. This is but our opinion or more specifically, our point of view. An operator on a team understands that all his teammates have a point of view, and that everyone's viewpoint is as valid as the next. (For an example of the phenomenon of multiple perceptions vs. one truth, I recommend the film 'Roshomon' directed by the master director, Akira Kurusawa.)

> *Life is a very sad piece of buffoonery, because*
> *we have . . . the need to fool ourselves*
> *continuously by the spontaneous creation of*
> *a reality*
> *(one for each and never the same for*

*everyone), which, from time to time, reveals
itself to be vain and illusory.*

-Luigi Pirandello (Autobiographical
Sketch, 'Le Lettere, Rome Oct. 15, 1924)

Early in BUD/S, our class was carrying on our heads, in teams of nine or ten men, large rubber boats that seemed to weigh a ton! We had been on the go with little sleep and were on the ragged edge of our endurance . . . or at least I was! One of my fellow trainees began whining aloud, *"I've got the whole boat! I've got the whole boat! Help me!"* The fact was, he didn't. We were ALL carrying the boat. (So I told him in more vigorous sailor language to shut up and keep moving!) From his perspective, which included his feelings of agony, he believed he was working harder than everyone else. From the perspective of ALL his teammates, he wasn't. Each teammate had, in fact, their own interpretation of the account. This is an example of multiple perceptions of the same incident.

---

 *To be extraordinary is to communicate clearly, distinguishing for others the difference between what you know to be the facts and what your perceptions are of these facts.*

---

When you take responsibility for your point of view and how your teammates might receive your communication, you create an enormous level of self-responsibility, credibility, and freedom for others to be themselves. Your conversations can take on a whole new level of credibility. There is a huge difference in how people hear you when you say, *"Listen, this is just my opinion or my point of view, but I think we're getting the raw end of the stick."* Rather than, *"We're getting the raw end of the stick!"*

*Just the facts, Ma'am*

—Jack Webb, as Sgt. Joe Friday,
on most episodes of the
TV series, 'Dragnet'

In BUD/S, we soon learned that any teammate not pulling his weight is hazardous to the entire team and the mission. Time is of the essence in performing each evolution with precision and success. Therefore the instructors and the trainees learn to communicate in a highly intentional way. This includes talking straight and making direct requests, although admittedly, the trainees experience little of this in the early stages! There is no time for lengthy, indirect conversations or candy-coated niceties that leave the other teammates feeling comfortable but ultimately wondering what is required. To be extraordinary is to give up your whining, sob stories and victimized perceptions that others are hurting your feelings, that their tone was a little too direct and made you feel uncomfortable. To be extraordinary is to accept and make direct requests of your teammates. It is to allow people to express themselves the way that they do, without you becoming victimized by their tone, and to simply listen to the essence of their communication.

Can you imagine Joe Montana, during one of his Super Bowls, walking up to the line of scrimmage, pausing, leaning down to his center and saying, *"Pardon me, Frank, but would you mind if I placed my hands under your butt? I'm not getting fresh . . . really. Does this offend you? Because if it does, I will try to be gentle!"*

People often withhold information, forgetting that they are members of a team. This is a form of controlling others. Withdrawal is deadly—to relationships, teams, goals and missions. Withdrawal and lack of communication among Navy SEALs can spell death to one's teammates! I'm not suggesting you blurt out information inappropriately that you know will hurt or humiliate another person. I'm also not suggesting that you indulge in your need to be childish and nasty. I'm suggesting you talk straight about the facts and be responsible for your delivery of the facts, separate from your perceptions of them. The secret to being an extraordinary teammate (an operator) is to be in full communication, not wandering around talking to yourself. You will fail many times before you even get to be a beginner at this secret. I speak from experience!

During one of my Vietnam tours, and in the days when only two SEAL teams existed, one on the East Coast and another on the West Coast, inter-team communication was not a regular occurrence. A SEAL working in my detachment was with his platoon of fourteen men on a night operation and seated in the forward compartment of an armor—plated Landing Craft Personnel, Light (LCPL) moving up the Mekong River. Suddenly, this SEAL's light machine gun fired on full automatic, spraying rounds of bullets throughout the compartment. The stock of the machine gun had been resting on the deck and the SEAL had been leaning over the barrel, thereby receiving the full brunt of fire. Even with the safety on, supposedly rendering the weapon safe, a pin keeping the stock and the main housing group together managed to wiggle free (evidently from the boat's vibration) thereby causing the bolt to release. The gun fired fifty to sixty rounds. The bullets ricocheted off the armor-plated walls. The one SEAL died instantly. Another SEAL was 'med-a-vac'd' and 'died' on the operating table a couple of times, but the doctors were able to revive him and managed to save his life. He is still alive today. After this incident I learned that a similar malfunction had occurred with the same model weapon in the other SEAL team prior to our situation. No one had been killed in that incident because the weapon's barrel had been pointing at the ground. Despite that incident, no one had taken the responsibility to communicate this information regarding the malfunction through the chain of command to my SEAL team. This lack of communication proved deadly.

If you look into your life, you will see that you are already on a number of teams and might not be relating to them in this way. Discovering all the teams in your life will provide you with a powerful place from which to operate. Where are you committed to accomplishing goals but have yet to succeed? Maybe the missing element is team. You might just need a team to fulfill your commitment and to support your goals. The choice is yours.

# Evolution for Career:

Read this chapter again.

**Purpose of Evolution:** To have you create powerful conversations with your teammates that bring about satisfaction.

**Action:** Starting right now . . . begin to communicate and distinguish the difference between your points of view about a situation from the facts about it in all your conversations with your teammates at work.

*Your Insights:*

## CHAPTER ELEVEN

# The Tenth Secret:
# Be Tough
# (It Is Not a Macho
# Thing)

# Chapter Eleven

## The Tenth Secret: Be Tough

## (It Is Not a Macho Thing)

*Courage is the resistance to fear, mastery of fear*
*—not absence of fear—*

—Mark Twain
(Pudd'nhead Wilson's Calendar, 1894)

You could say that this secret, 'tough,' is the essence of a Navy SEAL. It is only in being tough that someone can be unbeatable! This is an attribute possessed by most extraordinary people. To be tough is to be strong and resilient and able to withstand great strain without tearing or breaking. This is certainly true of Navy SEALs, but not only in the physical sense.

To be tough is not solely a male attribute. Women can and are, in many cases, tough, without being considered masculine. To be tough is an attribute that everyone possesses, but at their own level of proficiency. Women most definitely possess this secret physically, emotionally and intellectually. I may have survived BUD/S and three tours in Vietnam, but I've never given birth, nor have I been the primary foundation or force behind my children's upbringing! Their mothers have displayed, time and again just how strong and resilient—how tough—they are. Mother Teresa was renowned for possessing this secret.

To be tough is NOT the following:

---

- Pretending to be fearless.
- Withholding your feelings from others.
- Wearing the symbols (insignia, tattoos, gang colors.)
- Taking steroids.
- Shaving your head.
- Using foul and scatological language.
- Drugging.
- Owning a big pick-'em-up-truck.
- Ignoring society's rules or safety precautions.
- Showing everyone how much alcohol you can drink. This merely proves how much you can drink. It doesn't reveal how tough you are . . . and I had to learn this the hard way in my twenties!
- Fighting in bars.

---

Under the umbrella of success in any given field, you will find the leader of the team fully expressing this secret. To be tough means to play the game, whatever the game is, FULL OUT! Not acting like you are playing full out! This encompasses concentration on the job at hand and a focus on ALL of its details, moment by moment. To be tough is to be fully intent on fulfilling one's commitment, so much so that one is impervious to any adverse conditions or circumstances.

These adverse conditions can be physical, psychological and/or emotional in nature. Playing full out means playing the game without thought or hesitation.

In Vietnam, we frequently ran ambush operations to interdict (intercept) Viet Cong sappers who would be, in today's language, terrorists intent on disrupting the U.S. shipping route into Saigon. Our area of operation was a tidal mangrove swamp called the Rung Sat Special Zone. During these all-night ambushes, we would sometimes sit in water up to our necks along river or stream banks, waiting for the VC, who considered this their territory. If you asked an uncommitted person to do this for ten minutes you would hear him exclaim, *"Hey! That's a @$%#@&!*% crocodile over there!"* or *"There is something crawling up my leg!"* We remained quiet, in the swamp for hours, despite the presence of crocodiles and creepy crawlers. (We were more concerned with the AK-47-toting creatures who were hunting us.) In my direct experience, not one of the SEALs reacted with anything other than being tough. We were sometimes frightened. But like the roller coasters of our youth, we wanted to keep going out on these dangerous operations, taking our fear along with us. Writing my description of this now is akin to watching the movie *Rocky V* while living this experience was like going fifteen rounds with Muhammad Ali.

My mother, Rosemary, was tough. She played the game called, 'bringing up the kids,' full out. Her father had been killed when she was four years old, and at that time, she made a decision to be tough, which she shared with me years later. I learned from my mother to live the expression, *BECAUSE I SAID SO!* And I'm not suggesting that she meant this as though she needed or demanded her own way all the time. These four simple words—*BECAUSE I SAID SO*—judiciously expressed her commitment and steadfastness (her stand) in having our family be workable. Like a child, at the time, I just thought she was being unfair. Now I can see she was unwittingly training me to be a SEAL. To the outside world, Rosemary may have 'appeared' like the 105-pound former movie starlet who had worked with John Wayne and Buck Jones. In our house, however, she WAS the boss, and not to the detriment of her husband's masculinity or commitment. While I often lacked appreciation for this quality of hers when I was a child, I began to recognize its value in my life when I looked to see from which parent it had come. While some may describe it as a family trait or obtained through osmosis, the fact is I consciously began to employ this secret for my own ends until it just became a part of me.

Often, when someone is playing full out and is being intentional, others can mistake this behavior as anger or edginess. And this is no doubt where Navy SEALs unwittingly obtained their 'hard ass' reputation. This drive is not a by-product of edginess or anger; in fact, it is quite the opposite. It is while in a state of such extreme focus that the intentional person experiences peacefulness in the midst of action, in the face of external chaos and under adverse conditions—DESPITE HOW OTHERS MAY INTERPRET THEIR ACTIONS! On the outside, this drive might appear as one being stern or aggressive or cold. When a person is directing his/her thoughts or attention toward the job at hand and has clarity about their objective in the moment and is, at the same time, considering ALL steps (evolutions) and details required to achieve a desired outcome, there is no room to dilly-dally in emotions and feelings. Emotions and feelings are not part of the equation. In fact, when playing full out, emotions and feelings often require too much attention and energy and therefore hinder momentum. Back to our lioness . . . can you imagine Elsa, the lioness, telling her mate, Leo, *"Hey! Big guy! Give that roaring a rest, will ya? Me and the pride are a little fed up with your bossiness and language!"*

It is when we are uncommitted and playing haphazardously that we experience temptation for something other than our committed goals. Whenever people are faced with adversity, one foot is often found moving out the door while considering the option to break their commitment. This can sound like, *'Should I or shouldn't I?'* When this happens, we start to think about something other than our commitment. We think about how hard we are working or how we are not being appreciated. Or, we ask ourselves, *'Why should I be committed? I'm not getting anything out of it."* Our thinking gets us into trouble. When adversity strikes, our self-talk increases in volume. The problem is that the job of our self-talk is to dwell in our feelings and expectations about life. And when our feelings and expectations are NOT aligned with what is happening in reality, we decide that reality (in that moment) should get aligned with our expectations. In other words, people resist what is actually occurring in reality. When faced with adversity, most people would rather revel in their grand illusions about how life SHOULD BE rather than deal with the way life really IS. This often shows up in conversations, such as, *"My husband shouldn't be this way. Or, my company should be doing this or that."*

---

 *Life is simply what it IS and IS what it isn't.*

---

When we are cold, we want heat. When the market plummets, we want it to flourish. If during combat we

SEALs experienced extreme cold or heat, we simply accepted it and focused on our commitment. To moan and groan about wanting the conditions to be other than they were would be ludicrous. It would have made our missions more difficult than they already were and would not have served us in any way. Being tough is simply accepting reality the way that it is and the way that it isn't. It is accepting that it is cold and being okay with the fact that it is cold. Being tough is also accepting adversity for what it is, using the secrets to get beyond it, all the while remaining focused on the bigger picture—one's commitment. It doesn't mean standing out in a snowstorm freezing your butt off posing naked for the Polar Bear Club's annual photos! There is nothing wrong with being uncommitted. Just expect mediocre or zero results!

---

 *Lack of commitment can best be expressed as 'shit happens.'*

---

People might argue that Navy SEALs do what they do because they are detached, cold-hearted or free from emotional involvement. Movie and television writers like to depict SEALs this way. Maybe this is a compliment, but it is hardly the truth. Being detached is an attribute of saints and gurus. That certainly isn't the case when you are talking about the men with green faces covered in swamp slime or crawling into someone else's cave in Afghanistan! Anyone committed to something greater than oneself, such as defending one's country, is highly passionate and deeply and emotionally connected whether they express it to anyone else's satisfaction or not. Remember the secret, 'to be committed?' To be committed is to be bound emotionally and intellectually and some might say, spiritually, to an idea, principle, course of action or to someone. It is to pledge, promise, or vow to SOMEONE ELSE. It is to maintain this bond you made of your own free will on a moment-by-moment basis. Navy SEALs are not detached; rather they are extremely attached— but only to fulfilling their commitment and achieving the desired mission or goal. Navy SEALs honor their commitments ABOVE their emotions and feelings. Any SEAL who is emotionally detached is a danger to himself and to his teammates!

Look into your life to where you are suffering emotionally. This might include being worried, depressed, frustrated, and angry, etc. In this area consider honing the secret 'tough.' If you feel as though you are working too hard or you experience defeat or fatigue, do you have one foot out the commitment door? If not committed, everything you do will feel like a chore, or like hard work, or even feel like a hopeless pursuit. You might not be playing full out, except in your own sob story! Being tough is an attribute you might want to polish to enhance your romantic relationship, your family situation and/or your career. If you find yourself criticizing others who YOU think are too edgy or aggressive, think again. Maybe they are just expressing this secret called, 'tough,' in its full glory! You just might be pointing your finger to deflect, defend or protect your own lack of commitment, laziness or scattered, disorganized behavior.

People who are successful in their field are tough, which is part of why they are successful. Those who are being tough are often considered the bad guys. In the media, Martha Stewart has been reported as being tough. The media likes to interpret 'tough' and associate its essence with terms, such as cold-heartedness or ruthlessness. Someone might very well be this way, but this is not the definition of tough. To be tough is to be strong and resilient and able to withstand great strain without tearing or breaking. A tough person, when not in the heat of action, might also have the capacity to be warmhearted, thoughtful, considerate and open-minded. Cold hearted and ruthless are interpretations projected on tough people by those who most likely have never committed themselves to something greater than themselves and played the game of life as though their lives were at stake. Michael Jordan and Larry Bird have actually been described by various media dilettantes as 'assassin like' which goes way beyond the idea of tough. The media's interpretation was an attempt, in my perspective, to describe some inner extraordinary quality possessed by these two professional basketball players.

If people in your life, such as your boss, are 'too tough' and you are making them wrong in some way or are seeking agreement for your point of view from others, or you have given up and are feeling bored or resigned, reconsider that you have another option. If you are interested in recreating your life as extraordinary, to be around tough people will provide you the opportunity to polish, within yourself, the secrets—commitment, steadfastness, toughness, operator, teammate and trainability. And if this doesn't interest you, then remember that your tough boss just might be the source that keeps shoes on your feet and food in your refrigerator. So, you are best to simply accept it.

If proficient at this secret, and others say you are edgy and aggressive when you are just playing full out, be responsible for your proficiency with this attribute. Express your commitment to your teammates. Share your desire to achieve the team's objectives. Let them know that they need not personalize your perceived insensitivity. You also need not diminish this quality. On the contrary, to be tough is an attribute for which you should be proud. This is also NOT an argument for you to abuse people verbally at home or at work in the name of being tough. Remember feelings and emotions thwart one's intentions. To abuse someone is a highly REACTIVE emotional state, and the opposite of tough. Be mindful that your spouse and/or co-worker also has the right to express their toughness in their own way.

Whether playing the game of baseball, family unity, or professional success, we all want the tough ones on our side, whether we admit it or not. We all want our teammates to BE UNBEATABLE!

## Evolution for Your Personal Growth:

Read this chapter again.

**Purpose of Evolution:** To have you be tough (strong and resilient.)

**Action:** Choose an area in your life where you say you are committed and are still holding back from playing full out. For example:

- In a romantic relationship.
- In exercising.
- In spending time with your children.

Get a mentor. Give your mentor a list of actions you intend to take to realize this commitment. Ask him/her to manage you in being accountable to fulfill these promises. Request that your mentor treat you like a teammate and do whatever is necessary to have you playing full out rather than pondering. If this fails, take action again, and again, and again. Remember, the point of this evolution is to build your emotional strength and resiliency.

*Your Insights:*

# CHAPTER TWELVE

# *The Eleventh Secret:*
# *Be Interrelated*
# *(A Key Ingredient in*
# *Being Unbeatable)*

# Chapter Twelve

## The Eleventh Secret: Be Interrelated

## (A Key Ingredient in Being Unbeatable)

*A human being is part of the whole, called by us "universe," a part limited in time and space. He experiences himself, his thoughts and feelings as something separated from the rest—a kind of optical delusion of his consciousness.*
*This delusion is a kind of prison for us, restricting us to our personal desires and to affection for a few persons nearest to us. Our task must be to free ourselves from this prison by widening our circle of compassion to embrace all living creatures and the whole of nature in its beauty.*

—Albert Einstein

To be interrelated is to be connected with the forces and people OUTSIDE your immediate teams.

Upon entering BUD/S, a trainee is mostly aware of himself and has a conceptual idea of what it is to be a part of a SEAL team. Through repeated failings, he learns soon enough that he must be an operator, someone who can carry his own load and support his teammates, and also be a worthy teammate. Being an operator and a worthy teammate allows one to survive and SOMETIMES thrive. To be extraordinary is to realize that to thrive in the face of unbeatable odds on a sustained basis, you will need to be connected to the forces and people outside your immediate teams. This is the secret, 'to be interrelated.' SEALs discover this secret first hand, while training, and, on a deeper level, on operational missions.

To grasp this secret, look into your immediate surroundings and life. Where are you in or out of communication or partnership with others outside your teams? When you look at your life through the microscope called 'interrelatedness' you may find that you have reduced your life to the bare minimum of relating to others only when necessary to get by and to be comfortable. As Einstein says, *"This delusion is a kind of prison for us, restricting us to our personal desires and to affection for a few persons nearest to us."* Getting by is not thriving; it is merely surviving and being comfortable. And we all know where being comfortable leaves us . . .

I'm sure you have heard the saying, 'If, by the end of your life, you can count the number of your good friends on one hand, you'll be a fortunate soul indeed.' It is the sort of saying that can annoy the hell out of you if you are into living an interrelated life. Throughout our lives, we meet thousands of people. We are given the opportunity daily to be interrelated with many people, to see the world as one large family unit. Why is it that by the end of our lives, we only have one or two good friends? (I mean people with whom we can be completely open and honest, unguarded in our communications, and who are not out to get something from us or us from them.) Why are our lives reduced to trusting and relating to only so few?

*No man is an Island unto himself; every man
is a peece of the Continent, a part of the
maine; if a Clod bee washed away by the Sea,
Europe is the lesse, as well as if a
Promontorie were, as well as if a Mannor of
thy friends or of thine owne were; any man's
death diminishes me, because I am involved
in Mankinde; And therefore never send to
know for whom the bell tolls; It tolls for thee.*

—John Donne

*Keep asking me no matter how long—
On the war in Vietnam I sing this song—
I ain't got no quarrel with the Viet Cong.*

—Muhammed Ali, February 1966

To be uninterested in this secret is to handicap yourself, diminish your life, and thwart your own happiness, goals and success. To recreate your life as extraordinary, you may want to expand your sphere of relatedness.

Shari and I have a friend in Quebec, Canada—a young, single mother named Nathalie Ayotte. While some women in her situation might consider themselves victims of their circumstance, our friend is proficient with the secret, 'interrelated,' and created an exciting future for her and her son, Gibson. What impressed us, beyond that she is a great, single mother, is her ability to be interrelated to a wide group of people and organizations, from her community and provincial agencies to musicians, artists, media and public relations experts, etc. Nathalie searched out all the government programs and associations available to single mothers in Quebec. With the support of others, she went back to school, obtained a diploma in multi-media integration, won an award for her portfolio in a multi-media contest and started her own business in developing corporate identities and multi-media websites. Nathalie possesses, among many secrets, a level of proficiency in being interrelated to people inside and outside her immediate environment, and so is able to not only survive, but also thrive and create opportunities for herself that many women, in similar circumstances, would never find.

SEALs, through experience in dealing with the unknown and the unexpected, consider the big picture. They depend upon and are in relationship with others outside their team, such as organizations around them, from the personnel that operate the boats, planes and ships delivering and/or extracting them to the civilian authority for which they ultimately work. Contrary to Hollywood depictions, the lone, foul-mouthed rebel is not part of the essence of a true Navy SEAL. BUD/S weeds out these hambones and keeps the foul-mouthed ones who are team players and who are proficient with the secret, 'interrelatedness!'

During the Vietnam War, the close relationship SEALs had with their supporting units, as well as the professionalism of those units, frequently allowed these united forces to accomplish unusual missions that the SEALs could not have achieved alone—such as POW rescues.

On my third tour in Vietnam, I worked with an experienced SEAL officer named Bruce Van Heertum. While I was nominally his boss, Bruce had been in the teams for quite a while and had extensive experience. One day he told me he had received information on an operational Viet Cong POW Camp in the Mekong Delta. Supposedly, Bruce had learned that the VC were holding a couple of Americans and a number of South Vietnamese Army prisoners. In a matter of twenty-four hours, Bruce planned and commanded the entire rescue operation. He had coordinated with Naval gunfire support ships, with which we had NO direct contact (we were then working in a non-Navy organization), troop helicopters, and riverboats to support this operation. As a result of this operation, the South Vietnamese Army prisoners were freed, and the unit he commanded captured ammunition and weapons. (Unfortunately, the American prisoners had been moved out of the camp the day before, a practice for which the VC were known.) This was an extraordinary mission! To my knowledge no one, before Bruce, had attempted this type and scale of mission. Bruce conducted such an incredible and successful mission because of his strong sense of interrelatedness to many different forces with which he was NOT currently working. Two important elements created his success. First, he was highly intentional and personally responsible for creating and implementing the mission. He was committed and steadfast, an operator and an exceptional teammate. Secondly, he accomplished his mission due to his powerful sense of interrelatedness with the necessary forces to make the mission possible and on such short notice. This was NOT something he had been previously trained to do. This is an example of this secret— interrelatedness—at its best!

This secret can be applied to all areas of one's life. We have, by practice, become unrelated to our environments (meaning your relationship to people and to a much lesser extent the terrain.) For example, the highway system is designed to work for the safety of all who travel it. Through experience, we have learned that highways are not safe beyond a certain speed, and so speed limit signs are posted and enforced. And yet most of us have incurred at least one speeding ticket in our lives. When speeding, we are only thinking of our own need to get quickly to our destination. Speeding is a blatant example of our disregard for ourselves and the well being of others. Thousands are killed on highways each year. Statistically, speeding is more hazardous than any SEAL operation. Taking this one step further, I cannot imagine being on a hazardous SEAL patrol—which is all SEAL patrols—and having one of my men talking on a cell phone, or eating a Big Mac, or putting on make-up, or carrying his dog on his lap, or listening to K-Rock on full volume! And yet these are commonly accepted practices while driving, let alone speeding.

You can view your personal life through the interrelated microscope as well. If you are married and have reasons to avoid, ignore or even despise your spouse's family, this will affect your direct relationship with your spouse to the same degree—whether you are conscious of it or not. To be unrelated to your spouse's family, for whatever reason you have to justify your actions, is to dishonor an important aspect of your spouse. To dishonor others is to be righteous and ordinary.

To what degree are you interrelated to your career or work environments? If you are a financial advisor, for example, this might mean being in relationship to other advisors, to the governing bodies who set the laws for finance, to your clients and their families. The degree to which you are interrelated to your environments outside your immediate team is the degree to which you will be successful.

One's proficiency with this secret is directly linked to one's level of success on a sustained basis, especially in the business world. We often see people making it in their field, but how long do they remain on top? Donald Ziraldo, president of Inniskillin Wines in Niagara-on-the-

Lake, Ontario, Canada, is proficient at many of the SEAL secrets, specifically in being interrelated. He operates the most successful winery in Canada, which produces world-class wines that flourish in the region's cool climate, similar to the microclimates of France. Icewine, Pinot Noir, Chardonnay and Riesling are some of the wines for which Inniskillin has gained international success. At home, Inniskillin is a Canadian household name, and not because the company employs the biggest marketing or advertising budgets. While partner and winemaker, Karl Kaiser, is responsible for the quality of the wine, Ziraldo is the face behind the label. Among countless awards, he was honored with 'The Order of Canada,' a lifetime achievement award that recognizes people who have made a difference to their country. Ziraldo's interrelated sphere is so expansive that the thousands of people who know him consider him as one of their best friends. This is a grand title indeed and must be earned. So how is this kind of intimate relationship possible between ONE man and so many thousands of people? Ziraldo is highly proficient with this secret. With generosity of spirit, he creates and sustains powerful relationships with both men and women in countless fields—winery owners, artists, CEOs, skiers and snowboarders, and journalists in EVERY field, such as in wine and food, business, architecture, sports, art, etc. And more importantly, Ziraldo's sphere of interrelatedness spans across the planet. When visiting countries, such as Japan, China, U.S., Germany and Italy, to name a few, the citizens not only welcome him, but open their finest vintages and serve their favorite caviar. This secret has served Ziraldo and his corporation well.

You, too, can develop this secret to any level you like. Your interrelated sphere can be as expansive as you choose to make it. As you become proficient at this secret and your circle begins to expand, at some point you will have to give up doing the things that would have you injure or harm a person in any way. This includes any actions that damage or injure any person's physical being or emotional, psychological, economical, cultural or religious beliefs or states. (At this point, you could not be a Navy SEAL, for example, as you would be subject to orders that would require you to do harm to others.) Said in simpler terms, it is a matter of one's integrity as the highest expression.

You need only read the quotes by J.F.K. and Margaret Atwood at the beginning of this book to see that both were, and are, highly proficient at this secret. They RELATE(D) to this planet as one large interrelated family of human beings.

# Evolution for Family:

Read this chapter again.

**Purpose of Evolution:** To have you be interrelated in some area involving your children's lives.

**Action:** Build relationships in organizations that support members of your family and/or your family unit. Areas might be:

- Your children's schoolteachers.
- chamber of commerce or charitable organizations. (You might learn where you and/or your family could take part in volunteer work for others.)
- Talk to the neighbors and the police in your area to organize a neighborhood alert program.

The idea is for you to be interrelated, to practice focusing outward, beyond your immediate family, friends or interests.

*Your Insights:*

# Evolution for Career:

Read this chapter again.

**Purpose of Evolution:** To have you develop a new level of relatedness within your chosen profession.

**Action:** Write down a list of associations, divisions and/or areas in your field that you know exist, but with which you have no association. Build relationships in these areas.

- If you work in a large corporation, and you work in the sales department, consider learning about other departments of which you are currently uneducated, such as in marketing and/or in production.
- If you run your own business, develop relationships with other business people outside your industry but within your immediate environment. If you own a restaurant, for example, develop relationships with the businesses in your neighborhood.
- If you are a professional, such as a lawyer consider developing relationships with other professionals outside your profession, such as with dentists, doctors, accountants and financial advisors. You would be delightfully surprised to see the extent of which your business will grow in doing this.
- If you are an artist, develop relationships with other local artists or join an association that supports art in your community, city, state/ province, and/or country.

## Your Insights:

# CHAPTER THIRTEEN

# The Twelfth Secret: Be Resourceful (An Evolution of One's Skills)

# Chapter Thirteen

## The Twelfth Secret: Be Resourceful

## (An Evolution of One's Skills)

*Appearances often are deceiving.*

—Aesop, 'The Wolf in Sheep's Clothing'

*Tar-baby ain't sayin nuthin, en Brer Fox,
he lay low.*

—Joel Chandler Harris,
Uncle Remus and his Friends (1892)

A primary reason Navy SEALs succeed in the face of seemingly impossible odds is because they possess the secret, 'resourcefulness.'

What exactly is resourcefulness? With respect to SEALs, resourcefulness includes the qualities of one being capable, practical, simple, imaginative, inventive and improvisational. All operations, whether planned ahead of time at the base or undertaken spontaneously in the heat of combat, are comprised of these resourceful qualities.

The secrets continue to overlap. The first quality of resourcefulness starts with one being capable. Capability is an aspect of an operator. You can count on an operator being capable at his job. Operators do their jobs well because they have mastered the rules of the system, no matter what the system is. History reveals countless operators (extraordinary professionals) who first mastered, and then with capability and finesse, broke and reinvented the rules of their system or game—Picasso, Henry Ford, Olga Korbut, Stephen Spielberg, Barry Bonds, Michael Jordan, Ernest Hemmingway, etc. They didn't employ any new, good idea just to be different. SEALs don't break the rules to be rebels or to be different or to think outside the nine dots or box, naturally. It is in mastering the rules that they evolve in their skills to eventually perform outside the nine dots or box, naturally.

---

 *Breaking the rules is more an evolution of one's capabilities within the rules. Picasso was an operator.*

---

Picasso first learned how to paint at a fine arts school, evolved through his own Blue Period and Rose Period, into Fauvism, Cubism and into Modern Art, setting the standard, improvising every step along the way. Through practice, experience, and repeated failing, Picasso's capabilities evolved. This evolution is at the heart of resourcefulness. Picasso didn't begin this art form by sticking his 'ta-tas' in paint and dragging them across a canvas! He first mastered and was capable in his skills.

In the business community, CEOs and executives

are always looking for a new solution or a paradigm shift in their industry or are looking for ways to think outside the nine dots or the box, so to speak, to dominate their market place. Being extraordinary in one's industry need not be that ingenious or complicated. In one of my seminars, a participant shared with me, *"One of my clients is the marketing director for a mutual fund company. This company wants to create a paradigm shift in the fund industry with respect to marketing techniques used to market mutual funds to financial advisors and investors. What advice could I give him?"* This participant, over the course of the workshop, had shared with the group a great deal about her relationship with this mutual fund client. I had sufficient information to provide her with specific coaching. I said, *"Your client is wasting valuable time looking for that paradigm shift. It is not that complicated. Your client might consider turning his team into operators. In other words, have the marketing group show up at 9:00 A.M., instead of wandering in a half-hour late, still in search of the donuts! Have them master the details, and the shift will take care of itself."* She got the point. It's actually that simple.

If you are interested in finding new solutions or shifting the paradigm in your industry or profession, or you intend to stand above your competition, consider that you will need a team of operators capable of doing their jobs well, not a bunch of creative expressionists. With time, your teams will master the rules of their game, and like Picasso, skillfully evolve to a point where they are capable of breaking the rules with finesse, therefore creating projects that set precedent in your industry.

Another quality of resourcefulness is practicality. SEALs are practical. Once my wife, Shari, excitedly shared that she had obtained for us lessons with an instructor to go ice climbing (climbing up frozen waterfalls), just for the hell of it. I said, *"No! Thanks anyway."* Shari then said, grinning, *"What? Is my Navy SEAL afraid?"* I replied, *"No, I'm not afraid. I'm just not a retired Navy SEAL because I did foolish things in my life."*

The point is SEALS are practical. At age fifty-eight, climbing up a frozen water fall with no past training and for no particular reason is not the actions of an operator, but rather one operating with a few ornaments shy of a complete Christmas tree. Having made it through three combat tours in Vietnam, unscathed, there now has to be a damn good reason for me to risk my life. And climbing up a frozen waterfall just for the hell of it isn't one of them! This is not to imply that SEALs avoided foolish activities at times. Some did often, others at times. They weren't being SEALs when they were doing foolish things . . . more like eight-year-old boys showing off.

Another example of SEAL practicality took place in a training operation at an Army post. At the post there was a platoon of fourteen new SEALs and a company of Marine Reconnaissance totaling about 160 men, about half of whom had Vietnam experience. The Army, seeing a glorious opportunity for fun and entertainment, decided to have the SEALs and Marines engage in a boat race on a quiet inlet leading off a river. We used large rubber boats with a recommended capacity of fifteen men. The Army sergeants acted as the starters and referees. While I had worked briefly during BUD/ S with this boat type, I was more accustomed to the smaller, seven-man version. I had only participated in one rubber boat race three years prior, during BUD/S, and it was more of an endurance/harassment event than a race. All the SEALs had had various experiences with the boat. The Marines were excited, particularly their top sergeants, because it looked like this was an activity they were going to win. After all, their guys were studly looking, with big tattooed arms and little cigar butts sticking out of their mouths. We looked like an undisciplined mob of pencil-necked, rag-armed lightweights without insignia (this was part of our modus operandi in preparing for deployment to Vietnam. Wearing rank insignia only made it easier for the VC to choose targets . . . and if we were unfamiliar with our officers in a fourteen-man platoon, the platoon needed new officers!) The Marines' eyes glistened with anticipation upon realizing they had the advantage in manpower and strength! They grunted with enthusiasm in their manly Marine voices! They put about twenty-five men in their boat with no room left to squeeze in another soul. Talk about a warship! Talk about powerful arms at the ready!

I told four of my men to stay ashore and watch, leaving ten in our boat. The Marines continued to hoot and jeer at our 'motley' crew. A few Marines, however, looked puzzled, as if thinking, *"What are these idiot SEALs up to now?"* The race started and was over in about a minute. While we scooted along the surface like a water bug, paddling in unison, the Marines paddled in circles, swearing out loud and then, devolved into splashing one another with their paddles. While they took manly strokes, they had obviously forgotten Archimedes—one of the few lessons I had retained from the Naval Academy! Ol' Archimedes said that *"the more Marines you put in a rubber boat, the lower the boat rides in the water, and therefore the harder it is to paddle."* Our advantage was that our boat was free of Marines!

Kidding aside and as another aside, U.S. Marines are a group of extraordinary individuals with their own set of redeeming attributes. 'Courage' is definitely one of these, due to the missions they are assigned to and willingly accept. (During World War II the Marines' amphibious assaults across heavily fortified beaches throughout the Pacific took great courage.)

The moral of this story is that we employed a practical solution. Fewer men in the boat make for a lighter boat. How much more practical can one get? The lesson? Be an operator and be capable and practical, and then you can come across opportunities to be imaginative and inventive and stand out above the crowd.

One of the most important qualities of resourcefulness is simplicity. Simplicity assures fewer setbacks and breakdowns and provides opportunities for success.

*Simplicity is the ultimate sophistication.*

—Leonardo da Vinci

During my three tours in Vietnam, I heard about complicated and sophisticated operations that were also completely IMPRACTICAL, such as a daylight combat parachute jump into enemy territory followed by the influx of trucks to collect the parachutes! The only missing elements were bleachers, refreshment stands and the University of Southern California's marching band! The parachute jump wasn't a tactical imperative (a necessity); rather it was a way for some to qualify to receive Special Combat Jump Wings!

Here's an example of the genius of simplicity . . . one technique employed by certain SEAL elements on an infrequent basis was to travel to their jumping off point into enemy territory on a small civilian Vietnamese bus loaded with the local citizenry, their chickens and pigs. If we told anyone in the military at the time that SEALs were doing this, they would have said we were crazy or that it was suicide. (The former may be another quality of resourcefulness; the latter never happened.) These SEAL elements never encountered enemy ambushes and never lost a man, wounded or killed, using this simple insertion method. The U.S. government paid no extra money for a new deployment system. The Vietnamese on the bus probably thought that having Caucasians dressed in black pajamas and conical pheasant hats and armed to the teeth was the most exciting thing they had ever witnessed. People often like to complicate things. That's why simplicity can be ingenious.

Another quality of resourcefulness is being imaginative and inventive. Before being imaginative and inventive, SEALs utilized the secret called, 'interrelatedness.' To do the unexpected, SEALs first research and pay close attention to the details in operations conducted by the Army and the Marines or whomever else is involved on the 'friendly' side. Our role was to succeed when all other organizations and operations had failed or were unable to operate in specific areas. When we were called in to accomplish missions that appeared to be impossible, we looked at the patterns being unwittingly displayed by other U.S. forces to the Viet Cong. Our role was to see the big picture, to look for what had not worked in the past. In seeing this we could then be imaginative and invent ways to have our missions take the VC off guard. Our job was to be imaginative and inventive, do the unexpected, and not be regular troops.

The qualities of resourcefulness—being capable, practical, simple, imaginative and inventive—can be implemented in advance when SEALs plan their operations and missions. But they also need to be resourceful in the heat of combat and when faced with the unexpected danger. Another quality of resourcefulness that is used specifically in the field is 'improvisation.' SEALs know that every situation is unique. Training and experience can prepare the SEAL to a certain point. However, they also know the future is never what one expects. Knowing this, SEALs plan for contingencies or worst-case scenarios. And while they may do so, they KNOW they are never prepared for EXACTLY what will happen. Hence, they are READY to improvise! This is much like a classically trained actor who can improvise within the play whenever a fellow actor forgets his lines. There is a story about the famous actor, John Barrymore, who, while playing Hamlet and about to recite its most famous monologue, *"To be or not to be,"* noticed a stray cat wandering onto the stage. Barrymore strolled over to the cat, picked it up, and while petting it, delivered the monologue seamlessly. The improvisation was simple and brilliant. To be improvisational is to include everything in one's environment, not stop the action or complain when the unexpected arises. The longer you spend wallowing in your disappointment in things not going your way, or as planned, determined or expected, the longer it will take for you to improvise and therefore attain your goal.

---

 *Expect that setbacks and breakdowns WILL MOST DEFINITELY occur, and ALWAYS be ready to improvise. If everything goes as planned, it is a gift, not a given!*

---

So, to be resourceful, then, is to:

- Be capable in your job; be an operator.
- Be practical.
- Be simple.
- Be interrelated first, then be imaginative and inventive.
- Be improvisational.

If you are in business and want to dominate your marketplace, you will need your teams operating at the level of Navy SEALs in the face of ANY adverse conditions or seemingly impossible odds.

Of what, then, is an unbeatable character comprised? It is comprised of all the secrets. Disciplined, committed, steadfast, tough, and resourceful volunteers who know their lives are at stake, are willing to fail without being failures, willing to be operators, willing to trust their teammates as though their lives depend upon it, willing to embrace conflict, communicate the facts from their perceptions, and are interrelated with the folk outside their immediate team.

If some people in your organization and/or family are unwilling to play at this level of the game, it is perfectly acceptable. Their involvement would only obstruct your mission. Let them be just the way they are. Honor and respect them. It is NOT your job to try to change them. (I have regard for people who left the U.S. so as not to participate in the Vietnam War. They stood for their commitment, despite its unpopularity at the time. They certainly hindered no one. Besides, the USA was founded on, among other things, disagreement.)

## Evolution for Career:

Read this chapter again.

**Purpose of Evolution:** To have you be practical in your career.

**Action:** Look at areas in your career where your actions were thwarted. Examples are:

- I couldn't make it to the meeting because I had too much to do.
- I couldn't get the project completed because I had too many breakdowns at work.
- I didn't get the promotion.
- I didn't make my sales quota at the end of the month.

Pick one action that was thwarted. Write this action down on a piece of paper. Underneath this action, write down some possible courses of action you might have taken to obtain your objective. I realize that you cannot change what happened. However, if you don't look at what causes the failing, you'll keep doing it over and over again. This exercise allows you to see—objectively—where you might have gone wrong, which you may not have been able to see while inside the action itself. Professional sports teams look at, on video, the games they've already played to discover their mistakes and/or weaknesses.

*Your Insights:*

## Evolution for Family:

Read this chapter again.

**Purpose of Evolution:** To have you take simple yet powerful actions within your family.

**Action:** Apologizing to family members for your mistakes are probably the most simple, yet powerful actions you can take to develop your resourcefulness.

Another action might be for you to consider that . . . if you were to never see a particular family member again . . . what would you want him/her to know with respect to the contribution or difference he/she made to YOUR life? Acknowledge this family member from this perspective with the intention that this person NOT brush it off.

*Your Insights:*

# Evolution for Career:

Read this chapter again.

**Purpose of Evolution:** To have you be improvisational within your career.

**Action:** Create a simple action that is currently not employed that you could implement and save your company money. Examples might be:

- Start a recycling program.
- Join clubs, such as AAA or CAA that would offer your company or individual employees discounts on hotel rooms.
- When you are traveling for your company, out of town, choose the LEAST expensive hotel room. (Ask yourself this: *"Does my need to prop up my sagging ego justify my company paying extra money for my unconsciousness in a hotel room?"*)
- If you are not the CEO, propose an idea at a companywide meeting. Don't back down when the 'naysayers' or blusterers attempt to negate your initiative. Costing your company money is ordinary. Having a personal commitment to save your company money is extraordinary. And remember, WHAT APPEARS LIKE A SIMPLE, IMPROVISATIONAL ACTION IS YOUR FIRST STEP IN THINKING OUTSIDE THE BOX AND LIKE A NAVY SEAL.

## Your Insights:

# CHAPTER FOURTEEN

# *Conclusion: Graduation*

# Chapter Fourteen

## Conclusion: Graduation

*They wrote in the old days that it is sweet*
*and fitting to die for one's country.*
*But in modern day there is nothing sweet nor*
*fitting in your dying.*
*You will die like a dog for no good reason.*

—Ernest Hemingway

At some point during his career, the Navy SEAL comes to know who he is with respect to his relationship to the world. He possesses a quiet confidence, knowing he has mastered his skills. Having failed repeatedly, the SEAL arrives at a quiet place where he knows that no matter what the situation, under the worst circumstances, he will find a way to survive, succeed and excel. He will deliver results—whatever they might be—with overwhelming and lightning-fast impact. He knows he will get out of situations unscathed and move on to the next mission. In knowing this, the SEAL is at peace with himself, with nothing left to prove to the world—at least with regard to his craft. Most importantly, he knows what he cannot do.

Knowing thyself is a quiet confidence, not false confidence. False confidence is possessing certainty without having the skills or the experience to back this up. In briefer terms, it is known as being a BS'er. To a SEAL this attitude is recklessness. By virtue of their training, SEALs are cautious and vigilant. The ones who are not cautious and vigilant are either 'hanging with' Mr. Boris Smirnoff or Johnny Walker, or they end up dead.

## BALANCE IS PART OF BEING UNBEATABLE

Through having an unbeatable attitude and an array of attributes, the Navy SEAL knows he is extraordinary with regard to his craft. This is where things for the SEAL and other kinds of extraordinary people can get a little tricky. While the Navy SEAL might master his skills and be considered by many as extraordinary, his career is but ONE aspect of his life. The problem is people tend to focus so intently on mastering one specific game, such as their career or running their company, they often do so at the detriment of other aspects of their lives, such as their relationship to their romantic partner, with their children and families, or vice versa. (I learned this lesson, first hand!)

*Perpetual devotion to what a man calls his business, is only to be sustained by perpetual neglect of many other things.*

—Robert Louis Stevenson

While polishing the secrets will provide you with access to attaining greater success in areas in which you are already doing well and wish to thrive, my intent is that you also use these secrets for areas of your life where you are barely surviving. Areas of your life that do not work. The art is in creating balance.

Are you always in the doghouse with your romantic partner? Are you about to lose your job? Having trouble finding a job? Is your company on the verge of bankruptcy? Are you merely scraping by financially? Have you given up on your dream? Is this what's bothering you, Bunky? Take a minute. Be real. This isn't to depress you but merely to have you look at the areas of your life that do not work. It's to have you look at all the secrets so that you can determine which ones need polishing and which ones are dormant altogether. Ask yourself this: *"How workable is my life ... REALLY?"* And remember, the ideas in this book are to have you look, for a moment, at your life through a different stained-glass window.

I am committed that you have access to these secrets. Whether or not you use them is up to you. Remember you are ultimately responsible for recreating your life as extraordinary. There is no miracle cure. My commitment is that you use these secrets to master your LIFE and as importantly, to somehow use this attitude and these attributes to contribute to others.

Keep in mind that making a difference for others does not necessarily mean working for recognition in the form of citations and awards or striving to get your face on the dollar bill a hundred years from now. Remember, operators don't need to be the center of attention!

Making a difference for others is a moment-by-moment choice. In every moment, the universe offers countless opportunities for you to contribute your goodness and decency to people.

Recreating your life as extraordinary and making a difference for others is an attitude you can choose to possess one moment at a time. It is to be unbeatable! It is to be extraordinary as a matter of routine!

A man in one of my seminars said that he was so inspired by Mother Teresa's work that he left his career and home, traveled to India and willingly offered his services to aid in her commitment. Mother Teresa assigned his first job as getting up early every morning and, with a huge cart, travel the streets of Calcutta, picking up the bodies of people who had died during the previous day and night. How is that for a test of one's good intentions and desire and commitment to make a difference? He did it, and I considered him to be an operator. He did the job, as unexpected and uncomfortable as it was, despite the lack of personal glory or fame.

My commitment to make a difference in the world through my chosen profession as a Navy SEAL was tested in a profound way in 1968. That year I was privileged to be selected, along with twelve other Navy SEALs, to represent SEAL Team ONE, as the recipients of the first Presidential Unit Citation for a Navy command in Vietnam. We flew from San Diego to Washington, D.C., for the ceremony with President Johnson. As we walked into the room, there was everyone who was, in those days, newsworthy, standing around the room. I clearly recall thinking about how OLD they all looked! From my perspective, not a single one of them really KNEW or understood what we, the SEALs, were doing in Vietnam or what the Vietnam War was about, except from reports. I saw an immense gap of understanding between the policymakers and the fighters. This experience had me begin to question my commitment and whether any war was an effective means to reaching peace—if any war made a difference for my country or for the world. I questioned if my fighting was making a difference.

*Son my life is over, but yours has just begun.*
*Promise me, son, not to do the things I've done.*
*Walk away from trouble if you can.*
*It won't mean you are weak if you turn the*
*other cheek.*
*I hope you are old enough to understand.*
*Son, you don't have to fight to be a man.*

—Kenny Rogers, Coward of the County

This thought lasted briefly because I realized that this was the game I had chosen, and I was better at fighting than most anyone else. Besides, I loved what I was doing at the time. My questioning of myself did result, at that time, in my giving up the notion of nobility in what I was fighting for, however.

Before my retirement from the Navy in 1982, I sometimes wondered about senior retired generals and admirals who, upon retirement, suddenly worked for peace. After my retirement, I no longer wondered about this. I suspect General Sherman (Civil War) and General Eisenhower (WWII), for example, realized, like myself, that it takes no wisdom or skill to pull a trigger. In fact, it takes an enormous amount of wisdom and skill to be interrelated and communicate in the face of conflict without resorting to violence and to communicate with the commitment to bring about peace. Being at the heart of war, in the midst of combat and in seeing one's friends, teammates, countrymen and even the so-called enemy wounded and killed, is enough for any person with the dimmest wit and coldest heart to not only question one's commitment, but to experience the impact that violence and destruction has on all human beings. In my case, I realized the loss of just one of my men was not worth thousands of enemy killed—enemies I didn't even know well enough to hate! Enemies that are, today, our allies.

*Keep in mind that this is MY personal perspective and may not, in any way, reflect the views of anyone who has contributed to this book. Their views are their own.*

While I will always be an American by citizenship, I have declared myself a citizen of the world. I stand for people of all backgrounds, nationalities, races, creeds, and ethnicities having the right to live peacefully. I do not support the killing of human beings, at any cost or for any noble reason. Every person who has ever killed a fellow human being—INCLUDING MYSELF—always has a valid cause or reason for doing so. NO reason justifies killing a human being. As expressed so eloquently by Mark Twain:

*Man is the only animal that deals in that*
*atrocity of atrocities, War.*
*He is the only one that gathers his brethren*
*about him and goes forth in cold blood and*
*calm pulse to exterminate his kind.*
*He is the only animal that for sordid wages will*
*march out . . . and help to slaughter strangers*
*of his own species who have done him no harm*
*and with whom he has no quarrel . . .*
*And in the intervals between campaigns he*
*washes the blood off his hands and works for*
*"the universal brotherhood of man"*
*—with his mouth.*

These secrets are for everyone who is interested in recreating their lives as extraordinary and are committed to being unbeatable in the face of adversity and impossible odds. It is a peaceful process for men and women.

Let's take one last glace at what gives someone an unbeatable attitude and has them be one type of extraordinary human being . . .

Unbeatable people . . .

- Know their lives are based on 'free will.'
- Celebrate their uniqueness.
- Accept failing as part of the success process.
- Are disciplined (HIGHLY TRAINABLE).
- Believe most everything is possible and are AT WORK to fulfilling a commitment greater than themselves.
- Keep their word and are responsible when they break their word.
- Live as though their lives are at stake, accepting that life offers no guarantees.
- Are committed and revoke their commitments with honor.
- Are steadfast in their commitment.
- Embrace discomfort, knowing they are living life to the fullest.
- Do their job well and are trustworthy and dependable.
- Pay attention to details.
- Know their actions impact others.
- Choose to be on a team, and relate to their teammates as though their lives depend upon it.
- Talk straight without abusing or hurting others.
- Separate their perceptions from the facts and are responsible for their perceptions of the facts.
- Are strong and resilient (tough).
- Play full out.

- Accept that setbacks and breakdowns will occur and so deal with reality.
- Are resourceful—capable, practical, use simplicity, and are imaginative, inventive and improvisational.

# GRADUATION

Congratulations! You've made it through BUD/S and the TEAMS! Now that you have come this far in this process, and assuming you have stayed present through all portions of the material and have implemented all of the evolutions, YOU are ready to say whether or not you are unbeatable. Are you ready—RIGHT NOW—to recreate your life as extraordinary? Ultimately it is up to you to say who you are. Just like your life is up to you, so too is who you are in living it. Remember, stating that you are unbeatable won't make your life any easier. In fact the opposite is true. If you're intent on recreating your life as extraordinary—being unbeatable—be prepared to be uncomfortable. Now that you have the secrets, you have the tools, at least, to play a game worth playing, but one you have yet to master. When you play the game of life at the level of Navy SEAL, excitement and satisfaction will be routine.

If you've played full out in doing the evolutions, chances are you will experience at least one or perhaps a few of the following benefits:

- Increased effectiveness, such as more things go the way YOU SAY, instead of the way they are or it seems they are inevitably going.
- Inventiveness in areas where you hadn't been.

> - A newfound self-assurance and being powerful in new situations.
> - The ability to relate to people at a deeper level, not being stopped by your assessments, judgments and fears of other people.
> - An expanded sense of freedom, satisfaction and peace of mind.
> - The ability to clarify and sustain your commitments.
> - A newfound enthusiasm for life.

If you didn't play full out, that's fine. You can always implement the evolutions again and again and again, until you feel you have succeeded in them. Remember, as a SEAL, you're always failing toward success. And remember YOU are the only one who either chooses, in each situation, to declare yourself a failure or accept your failings and move beyond them.

However, if, after reading this book, you're still waiting for a sign from the man/woman above or to have some special feeling or for one of your orifices to take on a heavenly glow, or for someone else to anoint you as unbeatable . . . sorry, Bunky! You're treading water in the wrong ocean!

## —The End—

# Acknowledgements

I acknowledge and deeply appreciate the contributions of the following people and/or organizations whose support and coaching has contributed immeasurably to my life.

I was approached several times back in the 1970s about writing a book, but wasn't interested. This book took much encouragement and support by a number of people, some of whom didn't realize they were doing so.

## Team One:

Jack and Rosemary Schropp, my parents and the
first operators in my life
My brother, Michael Schropp
My sister, Jill Schropp
My aunts and uncles, particularly Jacob Leib

## Team Two:

My children, Kim Reese, Amy Heavey, Sarah
Caudill, Erin Schropp and
Christopher Schropp
My wife, Shari Darling
My three ex-wives, Diane, Ellen, Ginny

## Team Three: The Context Creators

Werner Erhard, a hell of a point man
The Landmark Education Forum Leader Body, staff
and assistants, present and past
Naval Combat Demolition Units, original members
BUD/S Instructor Staff and Class 31, East Coast,
1964
Richard Dolan

## Team Four:

UDT 22, 1964-1966; 1970-1971; and 1978-1981
SEAL Team One, 1967-1970

## Special Operations Team:

(The team that read, contributed and made recom-
mendations to this book or to the secrets)
Executive Officer and Ghost Writer: Shari Darling
Morale Officer: Stewart Esposito
Editor at Large: Michael Schropp
Ron Bynum
Tim Maloney
Tony Freedley
Nancy Gorsich
Kim Reese
Amy Heavey
Sean Henry
Donald Ziraldo
David Chilton
Elisabeth Wooldridge
Dick Grace
Sadie Darby
Brenda Bulgin
Laura Post

Tari Stork
Dina Robb
Alan Robb

# The Author

Jack graduated from the US Naval Academy with a B.Sc. in Electrical Engineering and has an MA in International Relations from George Washington University. He was twice the commanding officer of UDT 22 and executive officer of SEAL Team One. During his naval career he set and attained a new high reenlistment quota for all East Coast UDT Teams and developed many of the strategies and plans required for the rapid expansion and development of the UDT/SEAL team membership and capabilities. Jack made three combat tours and was decorated for both accomplishments and valor.

Jack has worked in the performance and motivation field since 1964 at which time he began a career of leading and improving the highly rigorous training and leadership programs for the US Navy Underwater Demolition Teams and Navy SEAL teams. He retired as a commander having completed a tour of duty at the Pentagon designing and planning the establishment of new and confidential weapons systems and concomitant training programs.

After retiring from the Navy, Jack attained extensive experience in the field of individual and group leadership training, having led courses for more than a hundred thousand people between 1986 and 2001 for the largest, off-campus educational company in the world. For this company he also led specialized courses for prison inmates, inner-city youth gangs and the Maori People of New Zealand, to name a few. From 1993 to 2000, Jack delivered consulting initiatives to *Fortune* 500 companies for LEBD, Inc., a San Francisco-based consulting firm providing large-scale organizational change and leadership development initiatives. Jack was also a consultant regarding security matters, including work with the staff of large public venues.

Today, Jack now designs leadership, coaching and team programs for corporations and organizations based on a unique system of decoding the Twelve Secrets of Being Unbeatable, and how they apply to business performance. This work promises that participants will have access to what it takes to become effective in the face of impossible odds in the business world—in much the same way as SEALS are effective in combat.

For more information on Jack Schropp, his programs, keynote speaking engagements and/or his book signings, go to: www.jackschropp.com